The Book Publisher's Handbook

The Seven Keys to Publishing Success

With Six Case Studies

Eric Kampmann

BEAUFORT
BOOKS
NEW YORK

Library of Congress Cataloging-in-Publication Data

Kampmann, Eric
The book publisher's handbook : the seven keys to publishing success with six case studies / by Eric Kampmann.
p. cm.
Includes index.
ISBN 9[illegible]5-0 (pbk. : alk. paper)
1. Publishers and publishing—United States—Handbooks, manuals, etc. 2. Books—United States—Marketing—Handbooks, manuals, etc. 3. Small presses—United States. I. Title.

Z476.K36 2007
070.50973--dc22

2007009057

Published by
Beaufort Books, Inc.

27 West 20th St.
New York, NY 10011
(212) 727-0190
(212) 727-0195 fax
www.beaufortbooks.com

Distributed by Midpoint Trade Books, New York
www.midpointtradebooks.com

PRINTED IN THE USA

10 9 8 7 6 5 4 3 2 1

Contents

The Second Key 13

Design and Format: The all-important deciding factors

The Third Key 21

Printing: Know all the basics

Introduction

Welcome to the turbulent and fascinating world of independent publishing. In some ways, now is the best of times for smaller publishers because the marketplace for books has opened up to include publishers of all types and sizes. It hasn't always been this way. Back in the early 1980s, a few dominant players on the publishing side (as well as the bookselling side) made it difficult for smaller publishing enterprises to squeeze in. But by the late 1980s, the ice on the frozen river of the publishing industry was beginning to thaw with a new set of opportunities that began to include publishers from every corner who may have started out with the humblest of circumstances and expectations. The climate was opening up for independent publishers in ways that no one anticipated.

Many factors came into play as the publishing world began to reorganize itself around some unmistakable changes.

First, technology played an important role, allowing publishing to become a guerilla business with ever more powerful and versatile desktops replacing the traditional office environments.

Second, wholesalers and distributors became more sophisticated in the depth and breadth of their services. As these entities grew and prospered, the independent publisher was in turn empowered in the trade book marketplace.

Third, the growth and power of the retail superstore proved to be an unexpected boon for the smaller publisher. The reason was simple, though few saw the implications at the time. Bigger stores with room for hundreds of thousands of titles could not possibly be supplied solely by the biggest publishers. The title void needed to be filled and the independent publisher was there, ready to play its role. It was a marriage made in heaven. Thousands of independent publishers were suddenly invited guests to the bookselling party and everyone, including wholesalers and distributors, was delighted.

Fourth, the astonishing growth of Internet booksellers represented a new "promised land" for smaller publishers. Consumers were now offered hundreds of thousands of titles they never dreamed existed, and the Internet booksellers began aggressively promoting these very same titles, whether they came from the biggest or the smallest publishers.

Finally, the flow of information over the Internet, along with cable television and talk radio, became the source of increased across-the-board book sales as authors, who never before had a platform, now became best selling authors published by companies that never would have existed twenty years earlier.

But what does this mean for you, the small publisher, in this time of great opportunity? For the most part it means you can now compete with the very best publishers as long as you can utilize the tools now available to even the newest and smallest book publisher. In this book, I have drawn together the key information you will need to actively compete at every level of book publishing. I call this the *Seven Keys* because I see the publishing process as a journey through checkpoints. Before proceeding to the hoped-for destination of a well-published book, publishers must first possess the knowledge, or key, from each crucial step along the way.

The *first* key is the editorial process. No book should be published without editorial input and direction.

The *second* key relates to overall book design and appearance. How your book looks, and what it communicates at a glance, can mean the difference between seen and sold and unseen and unsold.

The *third* key focuses on printing issues. How do you find a competent and responsive printer who will serve your interests? How many copies should you print?

The *fourth* key addresses the question of choosing the appropriate retail price for your book. Is your price competitive? Are you covering your costs?

The *fifth* key involves the all-important question of sales and distribution. How do you reach the trade book marketplace? Should you work through a distributor, and if so, how do you choose the right distributor for you?

The *sixth* key takes you through the marketing and publicity minefields. Marketing a book is like shopping at the world's most intriguing shopping bazaar; it is all there. But there is a practical limit on what you can do to sell and promote your book. Furthermore, there is nothing cookie-cutter about book marketing. Every book demands original thought and application. The decision on how you should publicize, promote, or advertise is a complicated one that differs from title to title. Marketing requires experience coupled with a sense of who the primary market is. Publishing means to make public; marketing is the method used to accomplish this.

The *seventh* key is a combination of the first six. You cannot be considered a publisher if you have not found a way to master each of the key publishing activities. This book is offered as an essential step-by-step guidebook that will lead you through the publishing process from key to key. It is my hope that the information presented here will make a difference and, in the end, your experience in this highly competitive business will be both profitable and enjoyable.

THE SEVEN KEYS

THE FIRST KEY

EDITORIAL
HOW TO GET THE EDITORIAL EDGE

EVERY BOOK NEEDS AN EDITOR

No book should be printed without the advice and consent of a good editor. A good editor improves a manuscript through objectivity and experience and is an invaluable asset for any writer. A quality editorial process can make a big difference in the ultimate success of the book.

Why expend enormous energy in creating a book when small mistakes can bring the whole enterprise into question? You need an experienced partner in the development of your book, another pair of eyes to aid you in making your book as perfect as it can possibly be. Without an experienced and involved editor, it is almost guaranteed that your book will be much less than you hoped for and sales may suffer, as your credibility will be called into question.

HOW TO FIND A GOOD EDITOR

If you don't have an editor on staff, ask your colleagues, agents you work with, and network within the industry. Editors at many houses may be charged with acquiring titles but might outsource the manuscript development and line-editing duties to freelancers. Your authors may have worked with editors who might be available to work on new projects. Your printers might also suggest people whom they trust and have worked with before.

You can find many capable freelance editors listed in *Literary Market Place™* published by Information Today, Inc. You can find out more out this company and their publications at www.literarymarketplace.com. Another source for finding freelance editors is the *National Directory of Editors & Writers for Hire* by Elizabeth Lyon. This listing of 600 freelance editors is by location across 48 states. It's available at Amazon and in bookstores throughout the U.S.

THE IMPORTANCE OF COPYEDITING AND FACT~CHECKING

The relationship between an author and editor is just one step in a successful publishing process. The line-editing of any book, fiction or non-fiction, should always go hand-in-hand with the determination to make sure that references to actual historical names, dates, locations, institutions, events, etc., are factually correct. These are vital bits of information that must be carefully reviewed whether a book is a novel, a biography, or a policy study. That is the role of the copyeditor and proofreader.

The human eye is a marvelous instrument, but when tired it can easily miss important typos or incorrect facts. For example, in a single uncorrected transposition, the Spanish Armada incident, famous as the 1588 battle in which England virtually destroyed a much larger and more professional Spanish fleet, suddenly becomes an event of 1858, nearly three centuries off; a similar lack of attention to detail can turn the New York City neighborhood of Rockaway into Rockaway, NJ, or ruin a perfectly good recipe along with the chef's reputation.

It is easy to dismiss the duties of copyediting, proofreading, and fact-checking as uncreative and tedious, but these functions are absolutely crucial to a book's credibility and should never be undervalued. Some editors believe that they can take on all of these tasks, but it has been our experience that a second set of professional eyes is a critical investment in the production process. Whether the author is writing as a novelist, historian, educator, entertainer, economist, celebrity chef, or from any dozen other perspectives, you should demand perfection in the fact-checking and proofreading. Anything they have written that will carry their name should be subject to scrutiny; their message and reputation will depend on it.

INDICES/APPENDICES

Indices are extremely valuable for non-fiction titles, particularly for works of history, biography, politics, economics, and science. They serve as reference points for researchers, teachers, columnists, book reviewers, and other interested readers, and are often the very first thing consulted by prospective buyers. In this way, they represent an entry point into the book itself, as important as the table of contents to many readers. It is even more important for those who will buy the book for specific sections of particular interest to them professionally.

The index is important to library sales for the same reason—as an easily-accessed research and reference tool. The index will show those most interested where the information most valuable to them is to be found and must be completely accurate. Many libraries will require detailed indices if a title is to be considered for their collections.

Remember that many online bookstore sites give authors and publishers the opportunity to post the Table of Contents or Index. In "the good old days," when books were only available in brick-and-mortar locations, the message behind clever chapter headings would be revealed to the potential reader by thumbing through the subsequent pages of the book. Now that stand-alone table of contents are posted online, and are read on-screen to aid in the consumer's decision making process, a "to-the-point" table of contents allows the consumer to easily understand the depth and breadth of the coverage.

Appendices are another attractive tool. Used effectively, they serve to illustrate and highlight reference points from the book and help readers and researchers to visualize facts, figures, documents, and other data that figure prominently in the narrative.

WHEN DOES EDITORIAL END AND MARKETING BEGIN?

One school of thought has it that marketing a book begins with the editorial, but it actually begins earlier, with the idea for the book itself and its subject matter. Each and every book, fiction or non-fiction, contains the kernel of an idea for the book's marketing strategy, and many books have a number of these so-called "kernels," from which an effective marketing plan or campaign can be designed. Editors should always be encouraged to work closely with their marketing colleagues when they are considering a project. Working together, they can bring the best book to market.

"THERE IS NO COMPETITION"

There is *always* competition, period. And EVERYONE is going to ask about it. Buyers are going to question sales representatives;

reviewers will scout the lists and often review similar titles. Producers will make their segment decisions based upon comparing and contrasting books and authors on a similar subject. Wander through a bookstore and note the dozens of "squatters," people perched on every imaginable surface, comparing books before committing their dollars. And, as anyone who has shopped at an online site will note, the online consumer, when offered an opportunity to supply a comment or review, will be only too happy to compare and contrast a book with their personal favorites.

An author's book may be the first biography of an obscure general of the American Civil War, but there may be five other books that discuss in a small section this obscure general and his works. There is always room for a new biography of an important figure or analysis of a subject, particularly when new information has been discovered, new documents made public, or newer value judgments made about the subject's importance or relevance. New cooking techniques demand new instructions for age-old favorites.

While the urge to feel that a book is completely unique may be comforting and seductive, it is shortsighted and even dangerous as a philosophy. There is always competition of some sort. Such an attitude might even short-circuit the development of a coherent marketing strategy by suggesting that there are no known plans that may have worked brilliantly for books even slightly similar. And if such plans do exist, it might well be possible to adapt them for your use.

Readers can be incredibly loyal to their favorite authors, but if they are making a purchase outside their comfort zone, they are going to comparison shop to discover the features or benefits of each title before making their buying decision. Good editors understand this drive and can help authors shape their manuscripts to meet the needs of a demanding public.

Establishing competitive benchmarks

A comparison of similar books can provide valuable information to determine where and how large the potential audience might be and how a strategy to achieve the best sales results might be orchestrated and carried out.

Editors should do much of the initial competitive analysis before manuscripts are signed. The good news is that much of this research can be done online, including reading some of the readers' comments about the competitive titles. Once they have identified their three to four most current key competitors, editors should be encouraged to go to a bookstore and "touch and feel" what the competition is doing—look at the packaging, pricing, features, and benefits.

Confer with librarians. Read reviews. *Library Journal* often compares and contrasts similar titles from a professional perspective, citing the key benefits and attributes of various titles. It is not only important to know what each book has, but to know what it doesn't have and how your title plans to address that missing information.

What are the hot buttons in the field? How do the competitive titles address these subjects? One significant way to get on top of the pressing issues is to review the most frequently asked questions in "Letters to the Editor" columns in newspapers or magazines covering a certain topic. Web sites, chat rooms, and relevant blogs can also be a great resource.

Communicating the competitive advantage

One of the quickest and most effective ways to evaluate and communicate the strength of a title is to prepare a competition grid that focuses on the following key areas:

- Title/subtitle and key selling lines
- Subject/genre
- Copyright date of competition—most up-to-date information
- ISBN, format, page counts, and price points
- Author's credentials vs. competition
- Features and benefits

Prepared at the time of acquisition, the competition grid should be updated when the manuscript goes into production and the sales and marketing groups begin to develop their sales strategies.

Sales and the competition

Through their relationship with accounts and various available sales systems, your sales representatives might be able to provide some competitive sales analysis of the author's previous titles or the recent sales of similar titles. BookScan, a sales reporting database, also provides an accurate snapshot of the retail-selling environment. Your distributor and/or sales team will be able to tell you more about BookScan and other sales-reporting databases.

The author as competition

When a sales representative first presents a new title, the buyer almost always looks at the history of the author's previous works even if they weren't published by you. It is important to know as much about the sales history of these titles as possible. If you are aware of anything that might have impacted the success or failure of an author's previous titles, it is important for you to provide the sales reps with an appropriate response to a buyer's question.

What is a "publication date"?

A lot of confusion exists around the concept of "Pub Dates." Some people think pub dates are unnecessary or have no impact on your publishing strategy, but we disagree. First, let us remove the confusion of terms. "Publication date" is not the same as "sell-in date," "bound book date," "warehouse date," or "ship date."

"Sell~in date"

Let's begin our discussion of dating with the all important "sell-in" date. This is the date that your sales representatives will begin previewing your titles to key booksellers. All of your sales materials should be prepared by this date. Typically this is six months before your book will reach retail outlets.

"Bound book date"

The "bound book date" refers to when the book comes off the bindery line. This information is most important for the warehouse. They will be anticipating receiving stock and preparing to cut invoices for the first releases.

This date can also be important for the publicity department. Reviewers and producers want to see finished books and publicists want to ship out the review copies as early as possible. They may request that finished copies be shipped directly from the bindery to the publicity office thus eliminating the delay of going through the warehouse process.

"Warehouse date"

The "warehouse date" refers to the anticipated date books will be received at your warehouse for shipment to accounts. Your printer should provide you with these delivery dates. This information is particularly important if you are creating corrugated displays or if your orders require special picking and packing. The warehouse needs to know when to expect inventory so they can schedule any special service details necessary before shipping the bulk of the orders.

"Ship date"

"Ship date" refers to the day your warehouse releases backorders and begins to ship your title to bookstore accounts, including wholesalers. If you are working with a distributor, "ship date" still refers to when orders start getting filled, but you need to be sure to supply your distributor with sufficient stock as soon as the books are available.

"Publication date"

The "publication date" acts as a signal to booksellers, reviewers, and producers that your books will be in stores and you will now begin marketing directly to consumers. At the publication date you should begin to advertise; media appearances should begin airing and display promotions should be up in participating stores. Another term you may hear is "on-sale" date. These two terms are virtually interchangeable.

Buyers note the publication date of your book at sell-in. If there is any significant delay to the publication of your title, you should notify your sales people immediately so they can contact their accounts.

How do I decide on a publication date?

The ideal publication date, which will maximize your sell-in process and support your marketing and publicity efforts, is six months after you first formally announce the title to your sales team. Once you have established your manufacturing schedule, you can establish a specific publication date—typically four to six weeks after the books have been released from the warehouse.

Is it important to meet certain deadlines for publishing my book?

The answer to this question is yes, *sometimes*. If your title is targeted for a specific holiday or event, it must be in stores at least two months in advance. For example, a Christmas book must be in bookstores by October at the latest. A gift book for graduation should be out by April. There are plenty of examples where timing is critical for a proper launch of your title. Work with your sales team to identify the key sales and marketing seasons and dates.

If you are planning to use your authors to promote their books, it is important to understand their availability to commit time to the promotion. You don't want to find out after the fact that your author has planned a family trip to Europe when you are trying to publicize the book.

Are all publication dates governed by specific deadlines?

Most titles do not tie into a specific date or season, nor should they. True, the big retailers want predictability, but still that does not tie you down to a certain month or time of year. The beauty of book publishing is that the perfect time to publish a book is when it is ready.

It's wise to take a deliberate approach to bringing your title to market. Get everything lined up, and then keep pushing. If you anticipate any significant delay (more than one month) in the publication of your book, notify your sales staff, distributor, and booksellers immediately. This is particularly important if you are participating in store promotions. With an early warning, they will work with you to accommodate a change.

Remember, you are only halfway home when you get to the publication date.

DO LARGE PUBLISHERS HAVE AN EDGE IN FOLLOWING SEASONAL SCHEDULES?

Independent publishers have a significant advantage over their bigger brethren because, unlike the staff at giant publishing firms, you are not tied down to an assembly line approach for getting the book out and marketed. The corporate mentality of large houses can be crippling to a publisher without the corporate budget. The smaller publisher has a longer runway, and if by chance the book is slow to take off, you still have plenty of time and space to launch without crashing and burning.

Yes, there are better and worse times to publish, and yes, there are necessary lead times for getting books into stores, but if you need a longer gestation period, take it. And if you need a year to properly market your book, take the year. Great journeys begin with small steps.

WHAT IS THE BEST TIME OF YEAR TO PUBLISH?

From late spring to late summer all eyes are on the very important fall selling season. Sales conferences, BookExpo America, and the fall catalog all point to high expectations for the entire list of brand new titles. Yet when the colors of the season have passed, the winds of winter become evident. If too much emphasis has been placed on the fall list, the winter will be long, hard, and cold indeed.

As December turns to January, bookstores and wholesalers feverishly begin to pack up overstocked books for return to sender. If your list of new titles is sparse come winter, you may experience a significant cash-flow squeeze. Therefore, it is important to spread your list of new publications over the whole year. January and February, for example, are strong months for finance and self-help categories; gardening titles sell well in early spring. It is always important to plan from a financial as well as a marketing perspective.

Publish no book before its time!

As the publisher it is your job to weigh the needs of the bottom line with the desire to bring the best possible book to market. Your editorial team will be charged with establishing deadlines and keeping your authors on schedule. There are times when you may have to postpone a title. It is far better to postpone a title than to publish an inferior book. However, there are authors, and we all know them, who just don't want to give up the manuscript. Only you can judge when it is time to say "pencils down."

THE SECOND KEY

DESIGN AND FORMAT
THE ALL-IMPORTANT DECIDING FACTORS

Weak, inappropriate, or bad design can undermine even the best-written book. A good publisher puts a lot of thought and energy into the overall design of the book, and especially into the book jacket. It's a shelf space business. How your book looks and what it communicates at a glance can make it stand out in the store, or get lost. Too often when publishers are contemplating a design, it's at a desk or on a convenient table, carefully lit without any other covers as a distraction. Standing alone, the jacket may work; but put it on a shelf with fifty other titles and its strengths and weaknesses will become very apparent.

While you are in the design stage, also consider how the cover will appear online. As important as it is to get the full cover design right, make certain it is also enticing when viewed in a much smaller size.

Do book jackets matter?

The obvious answer is that book jackets matter because they are the best and cheapest advertising vehicle you will have for your book. However, the obvious answer is not necessarily the only answer. You need to have a high-quality book jacket in order to be competitive. Does a good book jacket help get the book into bookstores initially? The answer is a definitive yes. The reason is clear to those who sell books everyday because we see the stacks and stacks of book jackets sitting on the buyers' desks ready to be accepted or rejected. Yes, in this environment, your book is judged by its cover.

Why are jackets important for the sell-in process?

Ideally, your sales team is selling your book six months before it is printed. However, you may feel your jacket concept just isn't quite right. Even though it might not be your final choice, prepare a "mock-up" of the most promising design for the sales presentations.

When your sales team presents your book to key book buyers it is important to have some "mock-up" of what direction you are going with the jacket art. This serves two important functions: First, the buyers have confidence that the book they are considering is going to be published. Having a mock-up jacket demonstrates that you are well along in the production of the book. One complaint we hear from buyers involves all the preliminary work they must do to order a book only to find out at a later date that the title has been cancelled. A mocked-up jacket gives them reassurance.

Second, buyers will give constructive critiques of the direction you are heading and will give invaluable advice on a number of book jacket elements such as: straight type versus an image jacket, colors, font style, etc. Don't miss this opportunity to solicit feedback from key buyers on your jacket concept. They enjoy helping in the publishing process and their expertise can be the difference between a so-so cover and a cover that really sells.

Does my book jacket need to be the best produced?

Your book is in direct competition with books published by all the biggest publishers. If your cover design does not measure up to the best, then the likelihood of it ending up in the buyers' rejection heap increases dramatically. So you need to have a professional designer produce more than one design concept for your consideration. It's also a good idea to talk to your distributor's sales people early in the process so that mistakes are minimized before those mistakes become expensive.

How do I find a good jacket designer?

Good designers are out there for you to find just like good editors. Jacket designers are often credited on book jackets. Many are independent contractors and might be available for your project or they can be an excellent resource for networking within the creative community. Use *Literary Market Place*™ or ask around; your sales people, your editors, and even your printers will be able to give you some names.

It's the spine

The same discipline, care, and concern you take in creating a selling cover needs to be applied to every aspect of the jacket. Although we all believe that our books will be shelved face-out, the reality is that most titles, unless they are best-sellers or in a promotion, are shelved spine-out.

So how should your designer respond to this reality of bookselling? What should be the most prominent information featured on the spine? What will resonate most with the consumer? Are the author's name and reputation of key importance? Make certain that you can spot that author's name across a crowded room. Do you have a clever title? Make that the prominent feature. Go with your strengths. Take every opportunity to deliver your message.

Cloth or paper?

The author wants a hardcover. Your sales department is telling you trade paperback. What is the right format? It all depends. If authors have developed a loyal following, and their devoted readers want to be the first to read the next book, they might be willing to trade up to a hardcover format. Others will wait for the paperback. Keepsakes are in hardcover; beach reading is a paperback. Reference books are tomes; travel books shouldn't weigh down your backpack.

The two most important questions you need to ask are: Where do you expect to achieve most of your sales? What format is appropriate for that channel?

If most of your sales will be through traditional book channels, then you need to consider the competitive marketplace. If the book store buyers are telling you that this is a price sensitive market and that trade paper is the preferred format, then it seems the decision is pretty clear. If the bulk of the books are going to be sold at author business seminars or to libraries, then a hardcover might be appropriate.

Is there a correct trim size?

Standard book trim sizes, produced and printed at traditional manufacturing and printing presses, achieve the greatest economies of scale, and are therefore the most cost efficient and require less special handling. There are times when a title's content—especially highly-illustrated or gift titles—might require or suggest a unique trim or binding. Costs associated with these unique sizes will undoubtedly have an impact on the overall cost of manufacturing your book.

Also, oversized or unusual trim sizes could force a title to be displayed outside of the category, or relegated to a top or bottom shelf with other "unique trim sizes." You want to make every effort to have your titles displayed within appropriate categories. You have enough competition; don't make consumers search for your books.

There are, however, times when the retail environment will dictate the trim size. If your titles are going to be sold primarily through specialty stores—craft books come to mind—the only display opportunities might be in racks sized for magazines. Your trim size decisions are often dictated by the merchandising opportunities.

How important is the cover copy?

The best way to sell a book at retail is to have the sales person standing next to the consumer whispering about all of the special features and benefits to be found between the covers. Unfortunately, this will never happen. Excellent cover copy is the next best thing to hand-selling (convincing, in person, each consumer to buy your book).

Don't let the design get in the way of presenting your sales points. The back cover and flap copy, if available, should highlight the most important points setting your title apart from the competition. Use this space to sell the benefits. Excellent quotes, bullet points, and the author's credentials all help to establish the book's worth in the mind of the consumer.

Remember, the back cover must include the ISBN, EAN, and all other appropriate retail price information. Designers who may not be familiar with book retailing requirements may try to hide or reposition this information so that it doesn't detract from the design. Designer preferences should never take precedence over practical and actual considerations such as positioning the bar code and ISBN on the back outside cover.

Interior design

Interior design can have its share of challenges. With the explosion of typefaces and font sizes, some designers love to experiment with a number of looks or design elements. Make certain the design works for the reader and that the typeface and size are right for the audience.

Author photo

When an author is instantly recognizable, or will be doing broadcast interviews seen by millions, then an author photo can be a selling point. Family photos from the last vacation have their place, but the author photo should establish credibility. Make certain it conveys information relevant to the text or the authority of the author. Use a current photo—if the photo looks dated, the consumer may jump to the conclusion that the book is dated.

If the author is not instantly recognizable or you have limited space, consider putting author information on an "About the Author" page in the back of the book.

Maintain your "data integrity"

Data integrity means making absolutely certain all of the information you print on your jackets, include in your sales material, and provide to retailers and informational databases (Bowker, Baker & Taylor, Nielsen, etc.) is correct. This information is the DNA of the book—the common thread that links the entire important sell-in and sell-through details. Accurate information guarantees accurate sales reporting to determine the title's profitability. One misplaced digit in an ISBN can cause a host of problems further along the way and can kill the momentum you are trying to establish for your book.

ISBNs (International Standard Book Numbers)

An ISBN is a 13-digit number that uniquely identifies books and book-like (booklets, pamphlets, etc.) products published internationally. For more information on the ISBN application process and proper use, go to *http://www.isbn.org.* The Library of Congress changed the length of the ISBN from 10 to 13 digits, effective January 1, 2007. This is an important change and affects both your frontlist and backlist. For more information, go to the Book Industry Study Group Web site: *http://www.bisg.org. T*o use an online calculator for converting ISBN-10s to ISBN-13s, go to *http://www.isbn.org/converterpub.asp.*

Check with your warehouse representatives to determine which ISBNs should appear on cartons. And make certain that your backlist ISBNs are updated when you reprint or revise.

EAN barcodes

In today's world, books must be scannable. An EAN barcode allows for this. ***Make sure you get the barcode right.*** An incorrect barcode costs money to fix and causes *lots* of headaches. Also, many national accounts require the retail price to be included in the barcode.

For a list of Bookland EAN bar code providers, visit the R.R. Bowker Web site: *www.isbn.org/standards/home/isbn/us/barcode.asp.*

Do I need to include library codes?

Library codes are required for books to be considered for review and purchase by libraries across the country. We recommend getting into the routine of requesting all of the appropriate retail and library bar codes for every title. By making this part of the production routine, you can be assured that your titles will have the opportunity to be considered for large, small and even special library collections.

For more information about the Library of Congress catalog card number contact their Web site: *http://www.loc.gov/loc/infopub/.*

Cataloging in Publication (CIP) Data is a Library of Congress bibliographic record prepared for a title that has not yet been published. The publisher includes the CIP data on the copyright page. The CIP data facilitates book processing for libraries. For more information contact: *http://cip.loc.gov/cipfaq.html.*

BISAC codes are another important tool in the bookselling and cataloging environment. For more information about the use of BISAC codes, contact the Book Industry Study Group at: *http://www.bisg.org.*

THE THIRD KEY

PRINTING
KNOW ALL THE BASICS

FINDING A PRINTER

There are a number of key questions you should consider when selecting a printer:

- Are they experienced book printers and what is their reputation in the publishing community?
- Can their staff and facility handle all of your special printing requirements (e.g. inserts, special trim, end papers)?
- Where are they located, how do they routinely ship to a warehouse, and what are their standard transportation costs?
- Do they have the ability to pack per specific warehouse or distributor instructions?
- Can they create and pack any special displays?
- What are their average turnaround times and minimums for reprints?

When considering new printers, ask about recent printing jobs for other publishers. While their own samples may give you a sense of the quality of their work, it is worth the time to visit a local bookstore and consider how those titles appear at retail. Check the printing and binding. Is it up to the standards required for your project? Look at the fit and fold on hardcover jackets. Are they within your acceptable standards? Are the trade paperback covers curling on the shelves? Are the boards warping?

Speak to your warehouse and customer service people. They are on the front lines of receiving and redistributing issues. They are often a great resource for key information about competitive titles and about how your titles are being received by the consumer. You need to know about issues early on and address them as quickly as possible.

If you are printing overseas you must not only consider the challenges of working with an international printer, but also anticipate the time and costs for shipping and customs from an international printer and the time and minimums required for a cost-effective reprint. There are also freight-forwarding charges once the books reach the port of entry and have gone through customs. If you are new to overseas printing, a reputable international printing broker can be an indispensable partner in the process.

Printing the right quantity

Selecting the best printer for your project is important, but deciding on the right quantity to print is critical. If you ask your printer, they are likely to suggest you print more copies rather than fewer because "Your unit cost will be lower." If you ask the author, he or she will generally want more copies because they intend to go out and market the title "everywhere." And if you ask your distributor (if you have one), they will return the favor by asking you, "How many do you want to print?"

Deciding on just the right number is not a science. Each title is different and requires its own unique set of calculations.

THREE BASIC RULES OF PRINTING

When deciding on the quantity of your first print run, there are a few general rules to follow.

First, be conservative. You can always reprint if there is sufficient demand, though you should be sure your printer can efficiently and dependably deliver your reprints in a timely fashion. This is particularly important during peak print times—especially during the late summer and early fall.

Read the printing and binding agreement's fine print regarding the over/under delivery of the requested print quantity. If the agreement has a 5% to 10% over/under clause, you want to make certain that you won't run out of stock if you are short-printed. Establish a printing order that is "no less than..." so that you are guaranteed to receive the minimum quantity that you will need to not only cover back orders but also sales rep and account samples, publicity review copies, author special orders, and other bulk purchases and reorders.

Second, if your book is aimed at the bookstore market, never print more than six months' anticipated supply. If you are reprinting a predictable backlist title, you might want to print up to a year's worth of inventory, but remember, you are tying up cash.

Third, use the sales history of similar books to judge your needs. Ingram's Ipage is a great reference resource for such purposes. If you have a distributor, they can provide you with access to key data.

How should you ship the books to your distributor?

Almost every warehouse has specific picking, packing, and receiving requirements that should be shared with your printer as early as possible. Most printers can handle these directions with little or no supervision. However, if you are using printers not familiar with book printing or you are using a non-traditional package or format, close attention must be paid to delivering the titles in a receivable condition. If your printer does not follow the warehouse's specific instructions, you are likely to incur extra charges and experience delays.

Once books are received in the warehouse they will be picked and packed to meet account specifications. All chain retailers have specifications with regard to the boxes that books are packed in. For example, Barnes & Noble requires that each carton be printed with the title, ISBN, quantity in the box, bar code, etc. If you are shipping books directly from your printer to an account, your sales people or distributor should advise you on this key area and you in turn will need to advise your printer.

Work with your sales people to identify any account-specific picking and packing instructions that are beyond the standard requirements. This could include promotional displays, clip strips, or other merchandising items. If they have the capabilities, you may find it more economical for the printer to pack to these requirements to allow for direct shipment to your accounts or quick delivery and turnaround at your warehouse.

Confirm and schedule all warehouse delivery dates. A visit to your distributor's warehouse will give you a keen appreciation of the nuances of handling thousands of titles being shipped to thousands of locations each and every day. The more seamless the procedure the easier it will be to meet all of your target publication dates.

It's true—there are times when things go wrong in the printing and binding process. Communicate any delays and changes, with anticipated new dates, to your sales and warehouse people as quickly as possible. This is particularly important if your titles are scheduled for in-store promotions. If your books have not been received in time to be staged for the displays, your books may not get into the promotion.

REPRINTS

Congratulations! Your title is selling and it is time for a reprint. You'll just push that button and...Not so fast. Reprints are not an automatic process and you need to be aware of a number of items when you are planning a reprint.

A number of publishers we have worked with in the past have been offered deals by their printer to print with an upgrade to the paper stock. The better stock was most likely excess special stock the printer used for another printing job. Sometimes, this can be a very attractive offer and you can get a great deal. However, when it comes time to reprint the title, the original paper may no longer be in stock or available. Publishers are then challenged to decide either to order and purchase the original stock at a much higher price and perhaps experience a reprint delay, or have to change the paper to an inferior grade to keep costs under control. Changing paper grades can create issues with stock color compatibility with the cover and binding. Both printings can end up side-by-side on a bookshelf, and the differences often stand out even to the untrained eye. And, in some worst-case scenarios, the jackets might have to be redesigned to accommodate a larger or smaller spine, creating additional costs that will eat into profits.

Make certain that any corrections or changes are prepared and submitted in a timely fashion for every reprint. If you are changing prices, make sure the ISBN and EAN codes reflect the change. You don't want to be losing profits at point-of-sale or spending money to sticker incorrect price points if the codes aren't updated.

If you are establishing a price increase, notify your sales people and key accounts. They need time to enter price changes in their systems and with the bookselling marketplace.

Reprinting the backlist? Have you updated to ISBN-13 and added the price code to the EAN?

The turnaround time on a cost-effective, simple reprint, with few or no changes, is about four to six weeks. Traditional book printers are usually well-equipped to handle a reprint in a timely fashion. And if your book takes off, you may be able to improve the turn-around times with your printer. Nontraditional book printers may not be able to respond as quickly to a request for another printing, or they may not have the paper and binding readily available. Factor these issues into your printer selection and ultimately your reprint schedule.

Staying on top of your sales to anticipate a reprint is crucial. Speak with your sales people and distribution company representatives before committing to a reprint. Inventory might be available at a wholesaler for redistribution, or there might be some returns that the publisher might not be aware of that could fill orders.

Finally, too often the final reprint decision is made in the heat of the moment, when sales at the retail level are slowing down. Be sure you know all the facts before you reprint because the last printing might cut into the book's profitability or even cause a loss.

Returns

Do you know how returns are handled at your warehouse? Are there price point indicators that automatically send any book under $16.95 to the remainder bin? Does your warehouse only restock from unopened cartons? Do loose books go into a destruct bin? Know the procedures; work with your distributor and warehouse to minimize the number of units that are considered unsuitable for reselling. Monitor your warehouse returns; move your processed shippable returns back into inventory as quickly as possible.

WHAT IF I HAVE BOOKS LEFT OVER?

Books depreciate faster than new cars, which is important to keep in mind if you are forced to sell overstock. Before you send books off to remainder dealers, consider other opportunities. Remainders are overstocked books that the publisher decides can no longer be sold at full (or even heavily discounted) price. Remainder dealers buy and sell books at pennies on the dollar. The author might be willing to buy back any excess inventory; there may be some special sales potential or an opportunity to donate to an organization. Under certain circumstances, excess hardcover inventory can be stripped and rebound into a trade paperback format. And finally, if you have exhausted all of these opportunities, there are a number of companies who purchase remainders.

THE FOURTH KEY

PRICING
MANAGING COST, PROFIT, AND MARKETABILITY

Pricing a book requires an understanding of what each book costs to make—so you get a return on your investment; what it will cost to promote—so that you can reach the widest possible audience; and what else is in the marketplace—so the price offers good value and is also competitive. Book sales professionals understand the market and its fluctuations. They keep in close touch with major retail and wholesale accounts, using them as sounding boards and sources of additional information. They use their knowledge to help determine the best price. Everyone wants to make money and have their book reach the right audience. Price is essential in making both happen.

Each new book is loaded with several direct and indirect costs that must be earned back over time through sales. The direct costs are made up of three components: pre-production, printing, and royalties.

Pre–production

Pre-production costs are often defined as one-time start-up costs. Typesetting, jacket design, and interior design are just a few examples of this kind of cost. Generally, this cost is considered fixed in relation to the number of books printed. Therefore, this cost, as a percentage of the book's total costs, goes down as you print more. It in effect disappears if you are fortunate enough to have more than one printing.

Printing costs

Printing costs are made up of three basic elements: paper costs, printing costs, and binding costs. It is true that the relative costs of printing can marginally decline with an increased print order, but it is also true that unsold books attack the bottom line. Print what you foresee needing over a reasonable amount of time, and as we indicated earlier, be careful before pushing the button on the printing.

Royalties

Costs associated with royalties differ greatly for different publishing models. For large, established publishing houses, this component represents a significant cost center for at least two reasons. First, they calculate royalty earnings based on the retail price of the book. Since the book is actually sold to booksellers at approximately one-half of the retail price, publishers are actually paying a royalty rate that is twice actual revenue. For example, if the royalty is fifteen percent of retail, the effective rate is nearly thirty percent of revenues from booksellers. This may work for the biggest publishers who often deal with high-visibility celebrity authors, but it is unnecessarily high for smaller independent publishers. The strategy for small publishers regarding royalties should be to pay a percentage of revenues rather than retail.

The percentage might be higher, but the cost is lower. Whatever your situation might be, be flexible and smart when it comes to royalties. Sometimes it might make sense to joint-venture a project, paying the author/partner fifty percent of the net revenues after costs. The payout for the author can be quite handsome if the book sells successfully. Second, large publishers often get in bidding wars for important authors, which causes a significant rise in the guaranteed advance royalty to the author. This is nice if you are a famous author, but for the rest of the world, it is not sensible to participate in this form of gambling. If a book does not meet sales expectations, the guaranteed royalties are still payable which significantly raises the royalty cost as a percentage of both sales and overall costs.

The three components of book production—pre-production, printing, and royalties—are often called "cost of sales." In other words, to sell a book, you have to make it, and these are the three basic elements of book manufacturing. As a benchmark of profitability, some publishers say that the three components should not exceed fifty percent of net sales. To the extent that a book does exceed the benchmark, the chances of a financial loss go up proportionately.

For more detailed information, we highly recommend that independent publishers read Thomas Woll's *Publishing for Profit: Successful Bottom-Line Management for Book Publishers* (Thomas Woll, 3rd Edition 2006, Chicago Review Press).

The information, templates, and forms Woll provides are invaluable for understanding the breadth of costs associated with publishing, distributing, selling, and marketing a book. Woll suggests ballpark figures to begin to develop a title profit-and-loss statement (P&L) and costs for a variety of sales and marketing activities. Obviously, these costs will change and fluctuate, but they serve as a strong foundation upon which you can begin to develop your P&Ls.

It is important to acknowledge and account for all of the fixed costs as well as the variable costs, for without a complete understanding of the financial realities of your business, it will be difficult to establish the parameters of profitability. Publishers need to evaluate the strengths of their organizations, decide what they can manage, and consider where and when they might need to turn to seek outside professional services for support. Once those determinations have been made, they can consider the other variables that impact a project and will ultimately help establish the retail price.

Establishing the retail price

There are countless variables to consider when establishing the retail price for a book: category; trim size; page count; hardcover or paperback; consumer or academic market; manufacturing costs; and royalty costs and payment structures. Marketing variables include promotions, advertising, and publicity. The general rule of those working at major publishing houses is to price against the competition. Another rule is to use a multiple of the manufacturing cost. The best approach is to ask your key sales reps because they have the best information from the major retailers and wholesalers who will play an important role in the success of the title.

Pricing from day one

In many ways, bookstores are the most difficult, expensive, and competitive places to try to sell your books, and therefore the publisher must be very aware of the pricing for similar books in the category. This means the publisher needs to take the time to research the competition by speaking with buyers, monitoring competitive sales, and strategizing with the sales team.

Begin to develop a competition grid when you acquire a title. This exercise establishes the key competition by subject, format, page count, price point, copyright date, etc. Much of this information can easily be gathered from a number of online retailer sites. With this information you can begin to develop a pricing strategy.

Throughout the publishing process monitor the competition. Add new titles and publishers to your competition grid when they are announced and watch for updated editions of older titles. A newly revised edition of a strong seller is serious competition. Note their promotional offers and marketing programs. What is it costing them to promote and sell their books?

The selling landscape can shift dramatically between the time a title is acquired and when it is published. Once the manuscript is put into production, review your pricing assumptions with your key sales reps. They will have the latest information from the major retailers and wholesalers. They can identify pricing and packaging trends before they become apparent at retail. Armed with this information, you can establish a competitive pricing position.

PRICING PITFALLS—WHAT TO LOOK OUT FOR

The retail price may or may not make a decisive difference with the book consumer, but bookstore buyers and buyers at the major book chains are very aware of price and often are very reluctant to commit to a title priced higher than its competition unless there are significant additional features, e.g. much longer page count, inserts, two color, etc., that warrant a higher suggested retail price and give the consumer added value.

Bookstore buyers are also much attuned to the marketplace and sensitive to the better selling formats within a genre. You may plan to publish a title in hardcover, but the bookstore buyer may suggest that the title might be better served in another format. Ultimately the decision rests with the publisher. You need to weigh the importance of the source of the information, as well as reactions from other accounts, and then make the best decision for your title. If you do decide to change formats and prices, notify your sales group immediately. Make all necessary changes to online and other industry source materials, and make certain that all bar codes and other price indicators have been updated before the book goes to press.

Pricing a title too high can hurt a book even before it is out of the gate. Also, remember that if a book becomes established and goes into a second, third, or fourth printing, it is possible to raise the price on a reprint. This is done quite frequently, but only if the book has an established market.

THE FIFTH KEY

SALES AND DISTRIBUTION
THE MARKET, THE PLAYERS, THE CURRENT TRENDS, AND HOW TO USE THEM

THE SELLING LANDSCAPE

The retail landscape has changed dramatically over the past few years. Main Street stores have given way to big-box retailers. Mall anchor stores have phased in and out, changing the consumer demographics of entire shopping complexes. We can shop online 24/7. These retail changes affect every type of business—including publishers.

With these changes came sophisticated sales tracking systems to provide retailers with the tools for profiling each location in their chain as well as the ability to tailor the inventory to meet the needs of the local community. Just-in-Time inventory allows retailers to manage their on-hand inventory, rapidly reorder fast moving titles, and clear slow selling inventory to make room for new titles.

In many ways, we have even more opportunities to sell our titles than ever before, but the bar has also been raised regarding selling practices. Publishers need to supply the sales team with the right tools to develop a partnership with their buyers and to successfully bring the titles to market. This also requires having the distribution and back-office systems and support in place to meet accounts' unique requirements.

Superstore chain bookstores

With the advent of the book superstore (30,000-60,000 free-standing square feet of selling space), the need for more books to fill the shelves has helped the independent publisher enormously. These superstore bookstores now have the space to stock a greater diversity of subjects than ever before. Independent publishers are generally on the cutting edge of genres and the superstores are supportive of your publishing efforts.

Barnes and Noble with 680 superstores, Borders with 300, and Books-A-Million with 150 are the dominant players in this category. They require approximately six months' notice for any book before it is printed. Communicate with your sales team so that you know months in advance what materials they will need to make the sales presentation a success.

Mall bookstores

B. Dalton with around one hundred outlet stores and Waldenbooks with hundreds of locations are the leaders in the mall bookstore market. With square footage of 3,000-10,000 square feet, they are more selective in the titles they will buy. Perennials such as *The Joy of Cooking*, the weekly *New York Times* bestseller list titles, and magazines are the standard stock they carry in most locations.

INDEPENDENT BOOKSTORES

Unfortunately, many of the mom-and-pop bookstores of ten to twenty years ago no longer exist. The superstore chains have dominated geographic regions and many independents have gone out of business.

There are, however, many excellent independents such as The Tattered Cover in Denver and Powells in Portland that have grown stronger with the increased competition. The independent bookstores can be proud that they "discover" writers and often help make a book a bestseller by talking to each other and their loyal customer base—classic word-of-mouth marketing often produces a groundswell that helps push a title onto a bestseller list.

DOT~COMS

The three major dot-com booksellers are Amazon.com, Bn.com, and Powells.com. The majority of other major accounts and specialty retailers also maintain an online presence. The beauty of the dot-com market is the speed and acceptance with which your books will be featured online. There are no "key buyers" per se who decide whether your book will be bought. Rather, there are "editors" whose main task is to insure that all data concerning a book is featured on their web pages.

When a consumer is drawn to your book through a review, word-of-mouth, promotion, or browsing and they click to buy the book, it can ostensibly be shipped within twenty-four hours. All three of the above dot-com booksellers have warehouses across the country and will generally stock a minimum quantity of every title.

It is important to monitor your own online presence with these accounts. Make certain that your final jackets are posted and any price or other informational updates have been made. Offer as much information online as possible to help sell the features and benefits of your titles to those late-night browsers.

Mass merchandisers

Wal-mart, Target, and Costco are the three largest mass merchandisers. They are very selective in their buying decisions, focusing on bestsellers, lead categories, and seasonal titles. If your book works in these outlets, it could mean sales of thousands of units. Many require minimum weekly per store sales rates to keep titles at retail. If titles don't achieve these thresholds, they will be pulled from the shelves, often resulting in disappointing sales and high return rates.

Everyone would like to see appropriate titles accepted by mass merchandisers and it can be accomplished with a sales team that has the contacts. It is important to work closely with your sales team, discussing the viability of your titles and the potential for your books selling through at these outlets. Proceed with caution because a big up-front buy forcing a larger print quantity can sometimes mean substantial returns and much-reduced profitability.

Book wholesalers

People often confuse book wholesalers and book distributors. Both are essential to a publisher's success, if not survival, but they differ greatly in the services they provide.

The book wholesaler should be seen as a service provider to bookstores. They do not create demand; rather, they efficiently respond to demand whatever the cause and whatever the title. They envision their task as serving the interests of bookstores and similar outlets, their main objective being to get product A to store B in the shortest possible time and at the lowest possible cost. Two of the largest are Ingram and Baker & Taylor.

THE LIBRARY MARKET: PUBLIC, SCHOOL, AND ACADEMIC

Ingram and Baker & Taylor, the two major wholesalers, ship to libraries. Others include Brodart, Bookazine, and Blackwell North America. It is important for you and your sales group to work with wholesalers to insure the "data" you submit to library processes is correct and timely. Everything from BISAC Codes to Library of Congress numbers are supplied to the wholesalers by your sales team.

Public libraries represent the largest segment of the library market. School libraries generally refer to kindergarten through high school, and book buying is vetted stringently for appropriate material. Academic libraries are found on all college campuses and research institutes and they generally buy only serious research works, books written by their faculty, or titles requested by faculty members.

Public library acquisition librarians make their purchases based on reviews appearing in publications like *Publishers Weekly*, *Library Journal*, *Kirkus*, and The ALA *Booklist*. These trade magazines will only review books **before they are published.** Most require a galley three to four months prior to the book's publication date if it is to be considered for review. A galley is an uncorrected proof of the text, usually bound with the finished cover. Ask your sales team for an example or explanation of what is required for galleys.

Many libraries compile category-specific suggested reading lists based upon reviews and their own circulation information. These lists are helpful when identifying your competition.

Who should sell my book?

Getting to the right buyer, at the right account, at the right time, and with the right materials is the key to a successful sales call. But the selling process only begins there. At the major accounts, most sales presentations don't end with an order in hand. Your sales team will get estimates while the buyers navigate through their company's purchasing procedures before they cut an order. The sales team will follow up—making certain that the orders are in-house for timely shipping and then monitoring the sell-through process. They will stay on top of the sales, communicating important marketing information to their buyers to maximize every selling opportunity.

For independent publishers, it often makes more sense to hire a distribution company. These companies not only handle all aspects of the selling process, but they have the contacts and reach to access all of the major sales outlets nationwide. They also ship, bill, collect, and handle customer service. These "back-office" operations are essential to the entire selling process and are best serviced by experienced professionals steeped in the bookselling process and retail and wholesale service requirements and expectations.

What is a book distributor?

Book distributors represent the interests and activities of book publishers. There are two primary functions of a book distributor: sales and distribution.

Why are distributors important?

Because of the explosive growth of the independent publishing community within the trade publishing industry, the role of distributors has become ever more crucial. There are several reasons for this: first, certain key wholesalers have decided to stop working directly with smaller independent publishers. Second, certain chain retailers insist that independent publishers use third party distributors as the way into their stores. And third, several distributors have become very professional in providing important selling and fulfillment services to client publishers.

Managing the back office

Running your own shipping, storage, and returns processing warehouse is both costly and difficult. In addition to managing the selling process, book distributors perform these warehouse duties for you, and have efficient systems for billing and collection in place.

Strength in numbers

In addition to their two primary functions, book distributors provide marketplace clout because they effectively represent many small independent and self-publishers in the marketplace as one entity. Unless you are doing more than $5,000,000 in annual book sales, you should seriously consider the distributor option.

What should I look for in a distributor?

As in any business relationship, you need to find a distributor whose practices and attitudes match your own. When you contact distributors, ask for the telephone numbers of some of their existing member-publishers. You want to have the most comprehensive picture possible of your potential business partner.

Visit their booths at trade shows like BookExpo America. Are the booths well managed? Are the sales representatives knowledgeable?

Find the right partner, and you have a much greater chance for a successful and profitable relationship.

Why would a distributor turn my title down?

There are really only three major causes behind a book distributor turning you away at the door. We think of them as the three "P's" of prospective book projects: pricing, packaging, and positioning. A large majority of the prospective book projects we see come to us with bad jacket and interior design, ill-conceived pricing, and no marketing plans. Distributors are not magicians and cannot take something poorly executed and turn it into a bestseller. Weak projects will most likely receive a "no" without further comment.

You are the publisher and responsible for the ultimate look and feel of your titles. You alone determine the pricing, packaging, and positioning. If you are willing to rethink these elements, consider some changes, you might be able to turn a "no" to a "yes."

What would help convince a distributor to accept my book?

There are several important and persuasive elements.

The first and foremost element is personal contact. Getting to the decision maker can help a lot. You need to persist in this because there are usually several gatekeepers standing in your way.

Second, references. It certainly helps if you have someone backing your project who knows the distributor (and whom the distributor knows). Your contact may be a consultant, a publicist, or an agent; if you can drop a name, it may help you get in the door.

Third, you need to have something to show off. Here, packaging is everything. If the book jacket looks like it could have come from a major publishing house, you will get more attention. If it looks like an inexpensive rush-job effort, you will get very poor results.

Fourth, how do you plan to get the public (your market) to buy your book? What is your plan? Whom have you hired to help you execute it?

Fifth, have you set a realistic publication date? Have you left enough time for your distributor to do a proper selling job on your behalf? Six months may seem like an overly long time, but in truth, it is just enough.

WHAT SHOULD A DISTRIBUTOR COST?

The fairest answer to the question, "Do these services cost too much?" is, "It depends." We believe the charges for distribution services should be *transparent* and *predictable*.

By transparent, we mean that "hidden" charges should be eliminated. Publishers should carefully scrutinize the contract, looking for extra charges for a variety of activities that might escalate their real costs. Issues such as return reserves, storage of books, returns processing fees, catalog charges, and other miscellaneous items need to be looked at and closely considered before you sign a contract. It is better to get these issues cleared up and laid aside early on in your relationship rather than regretted later.

By predictable, we feel the contract should have a single percentage for the distributor's fee, somewhere between 20 to 30 percent of net sales, depending on the annual sales volume of the publisher. If you're paying much above 30 percent, then you should look into the reasons. If you are a publisher with annual sales of $2,000,000 or more, then you will probably find you have a certain level of negotiating power.

When should I bring in my sales force?

Though the sales team plays its active selling role long after the book has been written, it should be considered a valued confidant and partner from the outset. The earlier the sales team becomes involved, the more valuable they will be to you. They can begin to monitor sales trends before they actually begin their calls for your titles. Usually, a professional sales team becomes actively involved about six months to a year before publication, during which time they can preview the book with key accounts and get valuable feedback. That is also when they begin to sell the book into major accounts.

How should I interact with my sales team?

If you are thinking of hiring your own sales force, keep the following three principles in mind. Are the sales representatives self-motivated? Is the sales force properly supported? Do they subscribe to the common purpose?

The first principle relates to hiring. If hired correctly, remedial correction from the management will be minimal. Work with self-motivated can-do people who will work beyond the call of duty to get the job done. Yes, there must be communication, but for the most part, as publisher, you do not need to interfere in the day-to-day activities of the sales reps.

Sales reps are called on to do much more than just sell. They are also on-the-spot customer service representatives, and they get frustrated and demoralized when not properly supported by the home office. Therefore, the second principle must be built around the idea of sales service support. Call it "customer service" if you will, but the motivation to accomplish tasks quickly and accurately must be instilled in every employee or service provider hired to support the sales team.

Finally, the sales reps must believe they are part of a sales team where the work of one supports the work of all. Sales reps can be "individualists" by nature, but management must work hard to make sure every representative understands they are part of a team. To the extent sales management can get reps to think in terms of "us" or "we," you will find a happier, more motivated, and more productive sales team.

These same principles apply when using a distributor's sales force, just not as directly. You will not be managing the sales team, but it is imperative for you to supply them with the proper level of support. If you will work with them, they will work for you.

SUPPORTING YOUR SALES ORGANIZATION

It is extremely important to have sales materials available as early as possible; complete with a defined audience, important author credentials, a comparison to the competition, and a blueprint of a marketing plan. Most of this information should be communicated on the appropriate Title Information Sheets—usually developed by your sales team to aid them in fulfilling all of the information requirements for their key accounts. Don't reorganize the title information template. It was created for ease in managing thousands of pieces of information. Consult with your sales team if you have any questions.

As discussed in the second key, every title presentation begins with the book jacket...it's a must-have. Also, galleys and sample interiors can be helpful to communicate the features of each title, and a table of contents can quickly identify the scope of subject coverage.

And last—but no less important—is a marketing plan. Buyers want to know how consumers will hear about your books and what will drive them to purchase. The next key will address specific marketing issues.

Should I send samples directly to accounts?

As often as possible, it is best to have your sales representative facilitate delivery of samples, bookmarks, and other promotional items. This is particularly important at the larger accounts where there are many buyers. You want to make certain your materials are delivered to the right people in a timely fashion to impact an order.

It's all about communication

I may sound like a broken record—I still haven't identified an equivalent phrase—but you must communicate, communicate, and then communicate some more.

Bring your sales team in as early as possible. Welcome feedback from the sales representatives and from their accounts. Keep them updated on changes and events that will impact the sales of your book. Ask sales management how best to communicate with them. They may establish an e-mail distribution list or request that all information go through one source. Follow their lead. Time is money, and sales people need to be focusing on sales.

Be specific. Your sales representatives are managing information on hundreds of titles daily. Make your communications actionable. ALWAYS lead with the Title, ISBN, Price, and Publication Date. If you are changing any of this basic information, clearly identify the change (e.g., Old Price: $16.95; New Price: $17.95).

Communication that is clear, concise, and actionable is the key to a smooth selling process.

From frontlist to backlist

The successful launch of a title will help secure its place on your backlist. Backlist sales are often the bread and butter of independent publishers. Always remember to mention an author's backlist when launching a new frontlist title.

Prepare a list of "like" titles to pass along to your sales team so that they can up-sell category backlist titles. You need to cross-promote your titles whenever and wherever possible.

How should I handle returns?

Having a quality product and a professional sales team can get your books to market. However, unlike almost every other industry, we have a family secret—returns.

Returns are a reality no one in the publishing industry wants to talk about. But like the proverbial uninvited guest, they keep showing up at the party and making their presence known.

Whatever your experience with returns, they are part of the book trade, so we need to understand and account for them. Books have been sold on a returnable basis since the 1930s when, in the depths of the Depression, some of the major publishers decided to offer accounts an incentive to take greater up front risks. We have been living with the aftermath of this innovation ever since.

Today, new titles generally experience a thirty percent to sixty percent return rate. Books stay on the shelf about ninety days and then come back if they are not moving at sufficient speed. The situation is even worse with mass merchandisers like Wal-mart and Target.

With backlist titles, the story is different. Here, returns run between 5 and 15 percent of sales. A very low return rate might suggest that you have too few books in the marketplace.

Don't forget to factor returns into your profit-and-loss analysis. For new titles, use thirty percent as a starting point, but if you are shipping more than 10,000 books consider budgeting for a higher percentage.

Special sales as a distribution strategy

Almost every book has a market outside traditional book channels. In some cases, sales to these outlets exceed what the book achieves in the general trade market. Examples include the gift market, premium sales, foreign rights, and proprietary publishing. There is a broad retailing arena to be tapped. If you work with a distributor, have a clear understanding of the markets and accounts they service. They are working for you, so don't duplicate their efforts. Rather, seek ways to reach consumers through other alternative sales avenues.

Special sales tutorial

Brian Jud, the author of *Beyond the Bookstore: How to Sell More Books Profitably to Non-Bookstore Markets*, offers some insights into the world of alternative sales channels:

> One of the biggest misconceptions among new authors and independent publishers is that bookstores are the only places to sell books. The best way to reach your final consumers may not be through the traditional system of distribution, but through nontraditional channels. It is estimated that half of all books sold every year are sold outside of bookstores. If you do not seek book sales outside of bookstores, then you may be missing half of your potential sales.
>
> A recent study by the *San Francisco Chronicle* lists book sales market share as the following: Large chain bookstores, 25 percent; Independent bookstores, 9 percent; Internet retailers, 12 percent; Book clubs, 15 percent; Mass merchandiser stores, 7 percent; Warehouse stores, 7 percent; and Other venues, 25 percent.

A nontraditional marketing strategy is the process of selling your books to individuals or buyers in businesses other than bookstores. Special sales, nontraditional sales, and non-bookstore sales are all terms defining these channels. If you have the time and the inclination, marketing your books directly to the people in your target markets can be both rewarding and profitable.

The essence of special sales marketing is the concept of segmentation, the act of breaking the market down into smaller pieces, each more relevant to your particular title. The total non-bookstore market is actually made up of hundreds of "mini-markets," each with varying degrees of suitability for your title. Segmentation helps you market your book where interested, prospective buyers congregate. Format, terms, and payment periods are open to negotiation. Books distributed to buyers outside the traditional bookstore markets are typically sold on a nonreturnable basis.

In special sales marketing, a successful title is often written in response to an identified need, is published in the form desired by the reader, and is then properly priced, distributed, and promoted directly to a defined group of prospective customers. You are not necessarily selling books; you are selling the intangible content of your title. Buyers are concerned with the relevancy of your content to the solution of their concerns, and the format in which it is delivered. This could be a book but it could also be a three-ring binder, a pamphlet, a DVD, or other packaging. When marketing to special markets, choose the segment first, and then choose the customers.

The Three Major Special Sales Segments

Specialty retailers

Special distribution entails selling to discount stores, book clubs, and catalogs—this means selling not only to the major clubs but also those venues dedicated to selling books in your genre. In the Special-Distribution sector of special sales (which includes warehouse clubs, airport stores, supermarkets, and drug stores) you will need to go through a distributor.

Selling to corporations

The second segment of special sales is Commercial Sales, which involves selling books to corporations to use as premiums, gifts, or incentives. They may use books as motivational tools for their employees, as gifts for their customers, or as premiums to lure new customers. Other buyers in the Commercial Sales sector are associations, schools, government agencies, and military bases.

Niche markets

The third classification of special sales is Niche Markets, which are significant groups of people sharing a common interest in your title. In both traditional and nontraditional distribution, you can sell fiction and nonfiction titles through distributors to resellers dealing with the consumer. While there is greater emphasis on personal selling in nontraditional markets, you still need to promote your works with press releases, reviews, media appearances, direct marketing, and sales promotional tactics.

How do I get access to potential commercial accounts?

Write to get a copy of the newsletters of groups or associations to see if they publish book reviews or articles by nonmembers. Do the associations' or companies' newsletters carry advertising? Perhaps you could write an article in exchange for advertising. Associations may sell through catalogs, on-site bookstores, at conferences, and on their own web sites.

The costs of selling through nontraditional channels

If you choose to sell through nontraditional channels, your selling and administrative costs will be higher, which will impact your profitability. In special sales marketing, it is your responsibility to sell to the retail outlets. Do you want to do that? You must also increase your expenditures for communicating to your prospective customers. Do you have the budget to do that? If not, you may choose to have your distributor undertake these activities.

For more information about special markets, you can contact Brian Jud at **brianjud@bookmarketing.com** or visit his website at *www.bookmarketingworks.com.*

Book selling today is a complex and demanding selling process. Professional sales people, working with the accounts daily, are on the front line supporting their publishers with creative sales solutions and responding to continuous market changes that impact the success and profitability of every title. Retailers and wholesalers are expecting knowledgeable back-office support, dependable customer service, top-notch distribution capabilities, and accurate, detailed accounting.

Now is the time to be as effective and efficient as possible. Go with your strengths and make certain that you have outstanding support in all of these areas.

THE SIXTH KEY

Book Marketing & Publicity Today

Find the Right Formula for Your Publishing Program

Marketing is a very misunderstood word when it comes to selling books through bookstores. With most consumer brands, marketing is based on sophisticated and expensive testing. Almost nothing is left to chance, which is not so much a guarantee of success as it is a reduction of the risk of failure. On the other hand, book launches involve little or no testing and therefore might be compared to a baseball batter taking a swing at a curve ball. If he gets a hit one-third of the time, he is considered a star. So it is with many trade books on a publisher's list. A few home runs pay for the missed swings. Larger publishers try to mitigate this situation by finding well-known authors who have previous successes, or barring that, they use the media as extensively as possible to create buzz and sales.

It is imperative to make the most of your money and focus your marketing and publicity efforts on the demographic that can most relate to your title. Your book is not for *everyone*—everyone does *not* need your book. Focus on your title's core audience and find the largest group of people who may be interested enough to explore your title further and ultimately buy it.

The Publishers Marketing Association offers many educational opportunities for publishers seeking marketing ideas and advice. You can contact PMA, the Independent Book Publishers Association, at *info@pma-online.org.* We encourage you to join this excellent organization in support of your publishing program.

WHAT SHOULD MY MARKETING PLAN DO?

The primary objective of your marketing campaign is to deliver sales at a profit.

To be a successful publisher, you need to develop a marketing strategy that presents a clear, consistent, and compelling message to engage every potential consumer to consider your title and close the sale.

Make certain everyone within your publishing organization understands your strategy. Encourage them to communicate this message in images and text, supporting every sales and marketing activity in the most cost-efficient manner. Everyone needs to be on the same page.

The most successful marketing programs launch titles on the frontlist and continue to support titles on the backlist throughout the life of the title.

When does marketing begin?

Ideally, marketing begins at acquisition. Too often, marketing is left to the last minute, but successful marketing is a long-term proposition. It commences at time of acquisition and should be constantly reviewed and refined throughout the publishing process.

Where do I start?

The four most important questions that every publisher should ask when acquiring a title are variations on the same questions the sales rep asks the editor, the book buyer asks the sales rep, and the TV producer asks the publicist.

- *Who is the target audience for this book?*
- *How will that consumer find out about this book?*
- *How is this book different from every other title on the shelf?*
- *Who is the author, and why should the consumer pay attention to what they have to say?*

The answers to these questions should be part of the acquisition decision process. Once a title has been acquired, the discussion begins in earnest and a marketing plan begins to take shape.

The successful plan first identifies the target audience—their demographics and psychographics. Where do they get their information to feed their interests? What newspapers and magazines are they most likely to read? What radio or television shows are they most likely to watch? Are their associations or professional organizations catering to the market? Are courses being taught? What are their favorite online destinations? Where do they shop, what formats do they prefer, and how much are they willing to spend?

The first resource should obviously be the author. Sometimes pulling this information out of them can be a chore. A well-conceived, detailed author's questionnaire can provide excellent information about the author's credentials, the target audience, project focus, and possible marketing directions.

Do all of my authors need to complete questionnaires?

The Author's Questionnaire is an important document that often gets overlooked or completed at the last minute. See Appendix C for a sample questionnaire. Some publishers won't issue that first advance check until they have a completed questionnaire on file. Others might give authors a bit of slack, but I strongly encourage you to have a completed questionnaire in hand at least six months before you intend to publish the book.

The selling strategy begins to develop nine months to a year before the book is published. The title starts to appear on publication lists and the sales group begins to look at their selling cycles and needs. They will need detailed information for sell sheets, presentations to major accounts, and catalog copy. The publicity department will be preparing trade announcement issue information and previewing the titles to reviewers and producers. The more information they have about the author, the more prepared they'll be to respond to questions.

Should the author help develop the marketing?

While it is important to keep authors focused on delivering their manuscripts, they should also be encouraged to view every resource, every contact, and every organization they encounter during the writing process as a marketing opportunity.

Several years ago someone developed an interesting approach to addressing this marketing question. Whoever it was has now passed out of the annals of history, but several of our colleagues have adapted the concept to help their authors focus on key areas. It is called "PENCILS," an acronym for a series of prompts to fuel the marketing fire.

Give each author a traditional questionnaire but also a notebook and pencil. Ask the author to complete the questionnaire within the first few weeks after acquisition, but to keep the notebook as a constant companion during the course of preparing their manuscript. The author is not to leave home without the notebook. Issue the following instructions: think "PENCILS" and make notes.

The PENCILS Method

P is for People/Publications

Who might endorse or review your book? Which talk shows hosts or celebrities are involved in your topic? Which publications might be vehicles for reviews or ads?

E is for Events

Are there topic-specific trade shows you should attend or where we might exhibit? Are there consumer shows where you might be able to interact one-on-one with consumers? Do you participate in any professional lectures or other speaking engagements which might be appropriate for additional appearances, and hopefully, direct sales opportunities?

N is for Networking

Are the movers and shakers commenting on your subject? Where have you read or heard them comment? They might be willing to provide an endorsement or blurb that can be used on the jacket. How can you communicate with them? Who hates your subject? Yes, there are times when a media person will comment that they "hate" something. Make a note, because if your book is about that subject, you don't want to waste a review copy. On the other hand, such a person might provide a lively and interesting interview opportunity for print, radio, or TV.

C is for Communities

What organizations, associations, and trade groups have active publications, meetings, Web sites, mailing lists, etc.?

I is for Internet

How are competitive publishers presenting similar titles? Do competitive authors have Web sites and how are they communicating online? What topic-related online sites do you visit? Do they have an online store? Which online sites review books or have online chat capabilities? What are the top blogs devoted to your subject? Who is blogging and what are they saying?

L is for Local Opportunities

All author activities should start in their own backyard. What are your favorite local bookstores? Do you know the owners or managers? Do they promote local authors? What about the top radio and TV shows in your local community?

List your local newspapers, magazines, and alumni bulletins. Do local colleges support community activities? What other local events reach your target market?

While sadly many local bookstores have disappeared, libraries remain an active destination for the reading community. Librarians are an excellent resource for finding more information about a topic; they are extremely knowledgeable about the interests of their visitors. Many develop and share recommended reading lists. Arrange to speak with your local librarians.

S is for Special Sales

What nontraditional accounts might sell your book? Are there stores that specialize in activities related to your content? Do they sell books?

By the time the authors have completed their manuscripts, their notebooks will be filled with ideas and leads...a timely resource for everyone in marketing and sales to consult as they develop their plans.

What is the role of sales in marketing?

A knowledgeable sales team should be an integral part of the marketing process. They can monitor competitive sales, pricing, and promotions, giving publishers valuable insight into successful campaigns. Get the sales team involved and consider their comments.

They will be expected to present your marketing plan at the time of sell-in and when they update their accounts on your activities throughout the launch of your book.

As publisher, you will decide which areas to pursue and which to table, but feedback from your sales group can provide excellent information to help you craft the most cost-effective marketing plan possible.

How do you develop a marketing plan?

There are five major considerations:

Distribution and sales projections: How many units are you going to ship, and how many do you think you can sell the first year?

Contractual obligations: Did someone promise the author a ten-city tour? Have you promised a full-page ad in a national magazine?

Is your author a confident spokesperson? Just because you publish their book does not automatically suggest that the authors will promote. Of course, the authors may have a different opinion about that. But, if you are planning to use the authors to promote, there are many options and expenses to consider.

Are there account promotions available? What is the level of commitment and what will it cost? Is this the right place to spend your marketing dollars?

What are your available dollars? What do you have to spend? Have you done a P&L? Are your sales projections realistic? What do you estimate for returns? Even though you have a budget for marketing, is it wise to spend it all?

What is the right marketing budget?

"Right" is in the eye, and wallet, of the publisher. Some publishers set their marketing budgets as a percentage of anticipated first year net sales. Typically this is somewhere between four percent and fifteen percent.

Some publishers establish a fixed dollar amount. "I have $100,000 and I intend to spend it all." That would be very nice, but does not happen too often. If you do have a specific dollar amount in mind, then build your program based on those dollars.

Other publishers develop a tiered approach—establishing a baseline dollar figure with money in reserve if the title takes off.

No matter which direction you take, when considering your marketing budget, spread your dollars based upon your decision to participate in the following marketing mix:

In-house sales support

Create a budget line for all of your sales materials—sell sheets, jackets, galleys and ARCs (Advance Reading Copies—another name for galleys), and catalogs. These are essential and the more professionally produced the better.

Giveaways like T-shirts, notepads, and other "stuff" are a fun way to draw attention to your books, but are they necessary? Not always. For giveaways to be truly effective, they need to be unique, humorous, or useful. Simply putting your book jacket on a t-shirt doesn't do it. Pose a crazy question and it might get worn. But will this get you one more order? Will it sell one more book?

Online presence

Are you developing an author/book-specific Web site? How often will you update? Who will create, support, and monitor the site usage and communities? What are the costs?

Trade Shows

Should I attend BookExpo America?

Many independent publishers feel they do not belong at BookExpo America. They opine that the show belongs to the big boys, that it is way too expensive, and that there is nothing tangible to be gained from it. Well, all of this is true in a way, but our experience with the show tends to override the negatives in some very important ways. We believe that BEA is one of the most important events on the publishing calendar.

What about you? Should you go? By all means—publishing is a networking business, and BEA has become a wonderful networking show. It is a great time and place to discover new markets, new sales opportunities, and make new friends. It can be an excellent source of information on what the competition is doing, and you can pick up promotion ideas. When possible, attend some meetings to learn more about the issues and opportunities in publishing today.

BEA has grown beyond the bookstore market. A wide variety of publishers and groups involved in domestic and foreign rights opportunities now exhibit at BEA. This is an excellent opportunity to think about the rights potential of your titles. Plus, major network show producers, reviewers, and other members of the press can be found visiting the exhibits.

Are there regional trade shows?

If you can't attend BEA, you might want to consider attending one of the many regional trade shows typically held during the late summer and fall. The American Bookseller Association Web site provides information on a wide range of events: *www.news.bookweb.org*. Attendance at one of these shows can be particularly helpful to launch your titles in your local region.

Review the ABA's programs for opportunities to address booksellers or consumers during roundtables or other organized activities. Consider hosting a small event, such as a breakfast before the show opens, to present your titles or meet with booksellers one-on-one.

Some organizations may sell mailing lists of attendees. You might want to purchase a list if you are considering some direct mail or promotional campaigns to accounts. You may even want to advertise in the show catalog or PW's *Show Daily*.

Promotions

Sell In

Do you need to offer a special discount or incentive to get your title into the store? Is your competition offering a more attractive program or special selling terms?

Displays

Are you creating special displays, shelf talkers, or other in-store merchandising materials? Many publishers announce these materials but cancel the programs if there isn't sufficient need or support from the booksellers.

In-store Promotions

Are your titles included in account promotions? What are your related co-op costs? With more stores preferring to create their own promotion programs, it becomes more and more difficult and expensive for independent publishers to implement unique in-store programs. Work with your sales force to identify potential programs that might be available to showcase your titles. Understand all of the costs involved and make an informed decision.

Store Signings

Plan, plan, plan, and then make sure you have locally publicized enough, because nothing is worse than showing up to an empty house. The chain bookstores have become very effective at coordinating events. They often have a "community coordinator" on staff.

Advertising

What will I get for my advertising? That question has circulated around publishing houses for years. Perhaps the better question should be, "How can I focus my efforts and advertising dollars to reach the most targeted audience?"

Do I need to advertise to the book trade?

Publishers assess the effectiveness of trade advertising in a number of different ways: as a branding ad for their publishing program; to announce major new titles of national importance; and to identify their commitment to key publishing areas.

Who reads the trade publications? Producers, authors, agents, foreign publishers, reviewers, the entire rights community, librarians, and, yes, the bookstore buyers.

You have a number of options to consider. Review the editorial calendars and see if there are specific issues that might be more beneficial to your publishing program. If you are working with a book distributor you may want to participate in their programs. But no matter what you choose, "close the loop." Make certain the ad includes the appropriate 800 number to reach your sales team and a snail mail or e-mail address to reach your company with any other inquiries.

BookSense

BookSense is the marketing arm of the American Booksellers Association, who provides a number of marketing programs designed to reach independent bookstores in a cost-effective manner. One favorite is the "White Box Mailing" that is mailed to over 500 independents across the country. You can include in this mailing advance reading copies, flyers, bookmarks, posters, letters from the editor, and other promotional materials. Bookstores look forward to receiving these mailings; the materials you provide help them to determine if your book is suitable for their store. If the answer is "yes," they will order your book from a wholesaler who, if the sales team has done its job, will be able to ship your book to that store the same day. For more information, contact Book Sense, Inc. at *www.booksense.com*.

What about advertising to the consumer?

While we're certain that your author would appreciate a full-page ad in a major newspaper or magazine, sometimes the best way to think about consumer advertising is to think small. Are there newspapers, newsletters, or magazines devoted to your subject areas? Bacon's Information, *www.bacons.com*, publishes the *Bacon's Media Directories*, which details the editorial needs of thousands of newspapers and magazines.

Once you've compiled a list of publications, visit their Web sites. Almost all publications provide editorial calendars and details about their advertising programs. A few hours of research might unearth a wealth of marketing opportunities. Also, you may find that the publication may sell related items—including books—on their Web site. This could be an excellent opportunity for additional sales.

If the publication has a book review section, you might get the coverage you want in a review and you can save your advertising dollars for another outlet. But if you can reach 30,000 targeted readers who subscribe to a publication that reflects their interests, it might be worth the expense.

If ad rates are prohibitive, perhaps the publication has mailing lists that might be appropriate for a direct mail campaign.

Publicity

There is an age-old adage, "Advertising is what you pay for, but publicity is what you pray for." That doesn't mean publicity is "free."

Publicity budgets need to consider the costs of preparing and mailing galleys, press releases, review copies, author tour expenses (including travel, hotels, per diem, media escorts, and props like posters and equipment), and other miscellaneous expenses. With a little work, a well-planned publicity campaign can get the book and author a tremendous amount of exposure. However, you are going to have to spend some money.

How do I begin to formulate a publicity strategy?

All authors want to be on *Oprah* and have their book reviewed in the most prestigious publications. Consider the numbers. There are tens of thousands of new books published each year. If TV shows were to have a book segment every day, they'd still only be able to cover 365 books a year. Most newspaper book review sections cover less than twenty-five titles a week. So what is a publisher to do?

A professional publicity staff can go a long way toward evaluating the opportunities and preparing the materials and the author to deliver the best possible publicity message to the most targeted audience. If you don't have someone on staff, consider hiring a freelance book publicist to shepherd your project through the publicity process. The "Public Relations Services" section of *Literary Market Place*™ lists firms that undertake book and author promotion campaigns. You might also consult with local bookstore community relations representatives. They work with publicists and might be able to offer some suggestions.

Early reviews

Many bookstores and libraries make their purchase decisions based upon pre-publication reviews of bound pages or galleys in *Publishers Weekly, Library Journal, Kirkus*, and *Booklist*. Most of these publications require galleys three to four months before publication. Submission guidelines, editorial calendars, and general information can be found at the following addresses:

Publishers Weekly
360 Park Ave. South
New York, NY 10010
www.publishersweekly.com

Kirkus reviews
770 Broadway
New York, NY 10003
www.kirkusreviews.com

Library Journal
360 Park Ave. South
New York, NY 10010
Chicago, IL 60611
www.libraryjournal.com

Booklist
American Library Association
50 East Huron
www.ala.org/booklist

ForeWord Magazine
129 1/2 East Front Street
Traverse City, MI 49684
www.forewordmagazine.com
This magazine focuses on reviewing titles by independent presses.

Read the submission directions and policies regarding inclusion and follow-up inquiries carefully. Too often publishers make the mistake of pestering the publications regarding the status of a review. Follow their guidelines; they will respond when appropriate. Remember to send along finished copies when they come off press.

Tools of the publicity trade

A good publicist will want to prepare a press release, comprehensive author bio, succinct message points, and visuals (author photo, jacket photo, etc., if appropriate).

These materials can be mailed or maintained as an electronic press kit on the publisher's and/or book author's Web site. Quotes or endorsements can be added to the materials as they become available.

Publicity "pitching" is very similar to an efficient sales call. Whether pitching an idea to a newspaper editor or radio or TV producer, the experienced publicist needs to deliver the message quickly and succinctly. How will this title and author educate, inform, or entertain the reader or viewer?

If you really want to communicate the essence of your book and author, improvise on the old elevator interview technique. "In twenty words or less, tell me about your book and author." No cheating. It can be done. And it should be done to effectively communicate today. Twenty words or less can start a phone pitch; engage an e-mail reader, and effectively sell your book and author.

Press releases announce to the world that a book has been published. They can be sent out early to reviewers and producers to announce the publication and should include important contact information for a review copy of the book or interest in an author appearance. They can also be sent, or a second release can be included, with the mailing of the book.

Producers' and reviewers' desks are inundated with dozens of books each and every day. While press releases or review copies delivered with home baked cookies or other accompanying knickknacks may be amusing and interesting, in the end, the producer/reviewer wants to know, "Why is the author an expert? What is new or noteworthy? What will my viewers/listeners/readers learn that will improve their lives?"

If your press release successfully answers these three questions, your book will at least be considered.

Review copies are the cornerstone of any publicity campaign. How many copies should you send out? How many can you afford to send out? The "low end" for most mailings is 100 copies. Even the smallest independent publishers will send 300 to 400 copies if they can identify "serious" targets. If the author wants to send samples to friends and family, offer a discount. Save your expense for qualified publications, media opportunities, and significant endorsements.

The author as spokesperson

One of the most difficult decisions a publisher must make is whether or not to put the author "on tour." Experienced publicists can usually judge an author's media readiness pretty quickly. They know what their shows are looking for and can judge if the author has what it takes to deliver the goods.

Publicists can set up a few small interviews, even some mock interviews, to test the waters. Speaking at a local library or to a civic group can help determine the author's comfort with public speaking. An audience Q&A period can help define and refine media talking points.

If media appearances are important, a publicist might suggest professional media training for the author. A media trainer can work with the author to get on message, to sit up tall, and to develop a comfortable and attractive media presence.

Successful media appearances can translate into sales. An ill-prepared author can be the death of a book. Producers monitor other programs, and if they hear a bad interview they won't hesitate to cancel an appearance. If the author can't stay on message and engage the audience, you may have to reconsider broadcast interviews.

Typical television interview segments run from four to five minutes. If an author speaks in paragraphs, not talking points, it might be smarter to concentrate on radio, where an author can take time to make a point and many interviews can be done by phone, eliminating all of the travel and entertainment expenses incurred during a tour.

Every author should be critiqued after every interview. Positive reinforcement and positive suggestions for improvement can significantly improve an author's delivery and ability to engage the consumer.

An excellent resource for authors who intend to promote through interviews on radio and television is Steve Harrison's *Radio-TV Interview Report*. This is a monthly magazine-format promotional piece that features authors who wish to be booked on shows. Hundreds of producers look through this monthly resource to find authors who might fit their format. For more information, contact Steve Harrison at *www.rtir.com*. Also, twice a year Steve Harrison sponsors the Publicity Summit in New York City where aspiring authors can meet key producers face-to-face. This is public relations networking at its best.

Events

Whenever possible, tie scheduled events into the author's own personal appearances. Work with the sponsoring organizations to determine if they wish to purchase books to give away or sell from the back of the room. If the author has an opportunity to sell at the program, think of providing a sell piece with the program materials. Alert your sales reps and local bookstores about these events. A good bookseller will often welcome the opportunity to create a small display carrying titles of interest to groups meeting in their community.

Local Book Fairs offer another great opportunity for the author to meet their audience first-hand. Contact your local bookstore or library about regional fairs. Think outside the book—an Italian food festival might be the perfect place to sell your travel books on Italy, or perhaps garner a speaking or panel appearance.

Are bookstore signings and events effective?

Years ago, publishers considered most bookstore related events to be a waste of time, particularly if the author was not a major celebrity. Times have changed. Today, most bookstores encourage events and even employ event coordinators. It doesn't matter if the author is well known or not. These events can often be extremely successful, but not always. There are a few rules you ought to follow in order to save yourself the embarrassment of having no one come.

First, work very closely with the store owner or event coordinator. Find out what works for them and follow their advice. Second, if you are doing an event in your hometown, make sure you invite people you know. Send out written invitations with a personal note. Third, if you are away from home, try to do the event after appearing on television or radio where you can promote the appearance. Fourth, make sure books get to the event location on time and, just in case, have a supply in your car. Finally, encourage the store to promote your book in-store at least a week before your appearance. This is grassroots marketing, and when handled professionally, it can help build recognition and sales.

Make sure to follow-up with the store after an event. Event coordinators and staff can give you an honest appraisal of the appearance and offer suggestions for improvement.

Web sites

Today, many publishers use their Web sites to sell more books—offering an opportunity to interact directly with the consumer, sell books, and develop an online community that could be tapped for future promotions. If you choose not to sell and fulfill directly, establish links with online retailers. Never leave a selling opportunity on the mouse pad.

Your corporate Web site should include a press room where you post all of your releases, backgrounders, and other important information about your company, your books and your authors. Include author appearance schedules—with as much detail as possible. Links to the author's Web site or blog can also be helpful.

Wherever possible, you should suggest to browsers a specific person to contact for more information. Don't let e-mails languish. Press people often contact publishers online and you may miss an opportunity if someone isn't checking these messages regularly.

Should the book/author have a Web site?

Building your own Web site depends upon your resources. A successful Web site isn't static. In an ideal world, where money is no object, you would love to be able to update your Web site daily, offering new information about author appearances, reviews, and fun things to do, like contests and quizzes. Weekly updates will keep visitors returning but you must keep them engaged. Web visitors have a short attention span. If they aren't intrigued and engaged, they will leave quickly and won't return.

Fan Clubs / Web Communities

If you are publishing a fiction series, a fan club managed over your Web site can be very beneficial. Create something people can and want to be a part of. Offer incentives, but make sure the incentives are of value to your target audience.

Blogs, or Web-logs, are another great way to build a community. They are easy to create, and if well-planned can attract interested readers. For more information about blogs, check out *www.weblogs.about.com.*

Direct marketing

Once the staple of many a publishing house, direct marketing has gone in and out of favor over the course of time. Many publishers are surprised to hear that a successful direct mail campaign is often a two percent response rate. That may not sound like much, but the ability to communicate with pre-qualified consumers is invaluable. Also, with direct marketing you can "test" a number of sales pitches and promotional offerings, discard what doesn't work, and build upon your successes to increase that response rate.

There are a number of magazines and online sites devoted to direct marketing. For more information, a good place to start would be Direct Marketing Market Place, 890 Mountain Ave, New Providence NJ 07974, or *www.dirmktgplace.com.*

The key to a successful campaign is a clean, targeted list. With over twenty percent of the population relocating each year, it is extremely important to work with a clean list and update it constantly. Compare list brokers; ask about their updating policies. Also, keep your own online address book updated.

FROM TELEMARKETING TO VIRAL MARKETING

With the introduction of "Do Not Call" lists, traditional telemarketing efforts have often moved to online activities. Online direct marketing is booming and when done well, can reach a targeted audience quickly and effectively. If done poorly, it can quickly be identified as spam and discarded. Viral marketing is telemarketing on the Internet. Online marketing should always be permission–based, giving the consumer ample opportunity to sign up or opt out.

WORD-OF-MOUTH

It's back...and it has become the big marketing buzz-word of the day. Publishers have found that well-planned e-mail campaigns or other viral marketing programs can be quite effective. Creative campaigns can be quickly passed along to family and friends, extending the reach of your message. A poorly executed campaign may never get out of the starting gate—or worse—be passed along with less than complimentary comments.

Remember—consumers are only too willing to talk about what they love and what they hate. Just a few years ago they would write a letter to an author or publisher voicing their opinion and expecting some type of response—a personal one-on-one conversation that rarely moved beyond their desk.

With the advent of e-mail, that quiet conversation has morphed into mass market communications. Readers will e-mail a publisher and copy everyone in their address book with their issues and concerns. They will offer their personal reviews in reading groups, they will review titles at online bookstores, they will comment on publishers' Web sites, and they will e-mail their cohorts and reach out to their favorite user groups and blogs.

If you choose to respond by e-mail, remember that your response can be forwarded around the world in an instant and can stay "out there" forever.

More About Internet Marketing

In 2005, 172,000 new books were published in the United States. With that many titles vying for the attention of readers and reviewers, it's hard to make your message heard over the din! Thanks to Amazon.com's Jeff Bezos, and the insight of other online retailers, small and startup publishers now have a way to sell their titles. But here's the rub: you've got to find an audience.

The internet allows authors to connect with their niche groups. Even if the author has written in a genre as broad as mystery, the groups are still out there on the internet, just waiting to be found. As more and more books are published within the various niches, the internet will become a much more significant way to sell a book than ever before.

Like Finds Like

There's a story that circulated in the industry about a book called *Touching the Void*. This book, published in 1998, was a harrowing account of near-death in the Peruvian Andes. The book got great reviews, but never managed to hit its stride. Then another book about a mountain climbing tragedy, *Into Thin Air,* became a huge hit and suddenly, *Touching the Void* started selling again. Soon, *Touching the Void* was outselling *Into Thin Air* and the publisher decided to go back and reprint this book, which spent fourteen weeks on *The New York Times* bestseller list. How did this happen? Internet word of mouth. People who read *Into Thin Air* recommended the other title at sites like Amazon.com and other online booksellers, and soon the buyers were getting both. The key here is that without this channel, no one would have been able to recommend *Touching the Void* except maybe to a few friends over coffee. But the internet gave fans of this book access to it as well as the ability to share their views.

Probably the most important piece of this is that the internet is a cluster of chatter; the key is to find the chatter that belongs to you, to find people who share your interests and get them interested in your book because, after all, it's what they wanted in the first place.

Building your site

The world is full of talented Web site designers, but more often than not, authors will ask their nephew or son to design their site for them. Now this is fine if your relatives *are* actual designers, but most of the time they have just bootlegged a copy of Dreamweaver and tinkered with it a bit, enough so they know their way around a little. Not enough to make them a full-fledged designer, but certainly enough to make them dangerous. They probably won't start blowing up small countries just because they hit the wrong button on Dreamweaver, but a poorly-designed site could cost a ton of sales.

Think of your site as a billboard

If you think of your Web site as a billboard instead of a Web site, you'll be much further along than most people. Why? Because people are surfing faster than ever these days. Studies have shown that the average surfer used to spend seven seconds on a Web site before deciding whether or not to click off; now they spend an average of one fiftieth of a second. That means that you have a snippet of time to prove to your visitor that your site is worthy of their visit. As surfers, we don't read, we scan, and the further we get down the road, the more we're finding that Web copy (the words on your Web site) isn't about writing; it's about writing less. We don't want to think, we just want to click, and preferably, we want to be told what to do. A well-designed site is not just one that's light on the copy, it's also uncomplicated and very obvious. Have you ever heard of the seventh grade education rule? Well, on the internet it's about a fourth grade education level. If you aim lower, you'll hit much higher in your conversion to sales. Now, surfers aren't stupid, not even close. In fact, surfers know what they want and won't be fooled or lured into something they're unsure of. The key to remember is that Web surfers aren't short on smarts, they're short on time, hence the shrinking window of opportunity to catch someone's attention on the internet.

When we're getting a site designed we have a tendency to want to push everything onto our home page. We cram it full of every piece of everything we've ever done, from writing a book to the time our little league team took first prize in the nationals. However, if you fill every inch of your home page with words and pictures and all the kinds of things that will send surfers scrambling for the exit button, they'll go into surf shock. That is when you land on a site that seems to scream at you from your monitor. The kind of site you can't wait to leave.

Making the sale

Once your sales copy is written, do NOT make your visitor search all over your site in order to buy your book! Put your BUY THE BOOK button in an obvious, easy-to-find space. You may be laughing now, but we've worked with authors who buried the BUY link so deep in the site it was impossible to find!

Get the word out!

If you're in the midst of your media campaign, don't overlook pitching bloggers, especially those who are opinion makers in your industry. Why? Because in the last twelve months bloggers have gone from writing online journals and opinion pieces to being newsworthy opinion drivers. In many cases, blogs are the most reliable places to get an accurate assessment of a news item, product, or service.

One of the main reasons blogs have taken this turn is because the public is increasingly distrustful of mainstream media and media outlets because these are often viewed as being somewhat biased and beholden to sponsors, organizations, and in some cases, even the government. Blogs and bloggers are beholden to no one because they are a free, unfunded source for media. Consequently, the public is turning their attention more and more to these bloggers, and media relations professionals are using bloggers to help them further their efforts by spreading the word about a topic related to a book/author.

So if you're convinced that bloggers need to be a part of your media campaign, what's next? Well, first you need to find the right bloggers for your story, and you need to remember, above all else, be honest and disclose everything. If bloggers find out on their own that there are parts of this story you didn't mention, they'll address them and this might cast a bad light on you. Bacon's Media Group recently published a report on pitching bloggers; here are a few issues they address (as well as a few ideas of our own) when going after a blog:

1. **Know the blog.** Don't just pitch randomly, know the blog and blogger you're going after. This means reading past blog posts—*all* of them.
2. **Don't worry about exclusives.** Bloggers love community and aren't hungry for the exclusive like the traditional media.

3. Follow the links. Most of the more popular blogs have links to other similar blogs; follow those links and check out those blogs because they might be worth a pitch as well.

4. Create your own blog. It's that community thing; bloggers like to see you've got an active blog as well and are a joiner.

5. Personalize. As with any pitch you want to personalize, don't send out a standard, generic pitch. Even truer than in traditional media, bloggers hate generic.

6. Understand the "blog food chain." Not unlike traditional media, the bigger the blogger the tougher it is to break in, so be patient, and when you're targeting bloggers, make sure you have a blend of first and second tier bloggers so you don't get discouraged.

7. Become a source. Once you've tapped into a blog, become a source for that blogger, even if it means turning a story over to someone more qualified. Try to stay on a blogger's radar screen with relevant tips, insights and news to keep the blogger updated on his or her (your) industry and help them make his or her own blog cutting edge.

8. Monitor the "blogosphere." Keep an eye on other blogs by tapping into blog monitoring services like Technorati (www.technorati.com) and Blogdex (www.blogdex.com). This will allow you to not only follow bloggers (who may not have RSS feeds which will allow you to see new content as it is loaded to the site) but also help you determine how many times your name and book has been featured in one of the blogs you've pitched (bloggers may not always tell you).

9. The mainstream media reads blogs. If you still aspire to attract traditional media airtime, know this: the media reads blogs and will often consider using "experts"—people who are featured on a number of blogs. Also, some bloggers might be attached to media outlets, which allows them to expand on stories featured in the mainstream media and offer daily updates on particular topics.

10. Finding news-driven blogs. While you're searching for topic-related blogs don't overlook news-driven blogs. These are blogs that vary in topic but are driven by daily news items. If you have a story that ties into a hot news topic these blogs might be the best place for you to go.

11. Saturate the market. Get your topic/story/book out there—as bloggers don't need exclusivity, you can go crazy with your pitches. But remember, the more saturated your category (for example: money, relationships, diet, and health), the tougher it might be to get those crucial bloggers' attention. We addressed doing a mix of first and second tier bloggers, but you might also want to consider doing second (or third) tier bloggers exclusively so you can build your reputation within the on-line market and use that as a springboard to up-tier to more prominent blogs and catch the rising stars.

12. Separate the good from the bad. When it comes to blogs nearly everyone has one now, so how can you find those first, second and third tier blogs while staying away from the "mom and pop" type blogs that can't really further your message? You'll want to start with a search on Google (search string: "your topic" AND blog) and begin reviewing the various blogs that pop up. Look for frequency in blogging (daily, weekly, etc.), tone, relevancy of material and topics/content addressed. A good way to determine this is in the posting. If the postings are all banter about recipes, family vacations, and other personal anecdotes sprinkled in with relevant on-point material, you might want to stay away from these. Why? Because good bloggers stay on-point, which also helps drive traffic to these sites. Bloggers who are just hobbyists and not opinion drivers will differ in their postings, and because of this, probably won't attract the level of traffic other blogs get.

A word about Google

Trying to get Google to notice you? Well, there might be a solution. There is a quick process you can go through to get a higher listing, some even say a very high listing, but Internet experts will caution you that your category can often determine where you fall in the ranking. Still, it's worth a shot. Head on over to: *http://www.smartzville.com/google-homepage.htm* for more information. To make sure that Google is picking up your website, add it at *http://www.google.com/addurl/*. To add your site to other search engines, go to *http://www.addme.com/*.

—Adapted from *Red Hot Internet Publicity: An insider's guide to promoting your book on the Internet* by Penny Sansevieri

Nominate your titles for awards

This can help with additional sales and also future books. Consider awards from the book community as well as those offered by organizations and associations focused on the subject. And when you garner that award, inform your sales staff and send out a press release. Many a reviewer will take a second look if they think they missed something.

Never stop marketing!

Wayne Dyer, who has sold well over a million books, still considers any day that goes by without a radio interview to be wasted. If you think you've finally "made it," it's time to keep pushing. When a title moves to the backlist, it often languishes without much support. Continue to seek opportunities to promote your lists.

There is no such thing as a final marketing plan

A good marketing plan sets the stage for promotional efforts but should be elastic enough to allow for change. It must set realistic goals, and manage realistic expectations. Don't be afraid of change. If the book is getting wonderful reviews, consider additional publications. If the author is great, consider more appearances. If the author isn't delivering, pull the plug on appearances. Build on your strengths; don't needlessly throw money away in unproductive areas when that same dollar can be used to build on the success of a winning title.

When all is said and done...

We are firm believers in doing a post-op analysis on every title that has a major marketing push—evaluating the success of the sales and marketing efforts at the end of a selling season. We should never be afraid to pat ourselves on the back for the things that worked well, and to honestly evaluate the activities that did not go as planned. We can often learn as much from what we did wrong as from what we did right.

Successful publishers apply what they have learned from these efforts to develop their future plans. Activities and opportunities will change from day-to-day but as long as publishers understand and respect the needs of the consumer and are willing to adapt and change with the marketplace, they will be in the best position to realize success and profitability.

THE SEVENTH KEY

The Publisher is YOU

At the end of the day, the keys are in YOUR hands. You have made the decision to be a publisher and, as a publisher, you need to place yourself at the center of the action. There is no other way to understand the role you have chosen to play. You are the maestro, the coach, and the head cheerleader. It is a great role and some are born to fill it masterfully.

On the other hand, it is a difficult role, and not everyone is cut out for the complexities of knowing every part of this puzzle and its many pieces. After all, some may be great editors, but have no interest in sales. Others may be marketing geniuses, but have no financial background. Still others may like to dwell on every design detail, but have little desire to learn about the book marketplace.

The publisher is not just an editor, a sales manager, or marketing person. He or she is all of the above and more. Every detail in this intricate tapestry called book publishing will challenge the imagination and mind of the publisher. But it is not just the publisher who is the hero of this story. Great publishers hire great sales managers, financial managers, and marketing and publicity managers, not to mention all the other key personnel to fill out their team. For in the last analysis, publishing is a team effort. Bestsellers often happen because a team of motivated people saw a book's potential early on and took a chance.

Once you have taken possession of the sixth key and you feel the journey is nearing completion, think again. The journey never really ends because now, after you have learned the elements of your trade, you are ready to be a publisher. The journey has taken time; it has cost you in sweat and tears, but every step has prepared you to really take on the role of publisher and feel comfortable and competent in doing your job. So congratulations! You have joined the ranks of other greats who have come before. You have done your homework; you have mastered your trade. Now let's get on with it. Let's begin the quest for the next great book, a book built by a community of professional and dedicated people.

SIX CASE STUDIES

Planning for the Unexpected
The Story of *All Creatures Great and Small*

I suspect I could tell everything I know about the publication of *All Creatures Great and Small* and still never mention some item or two that was absolutely critical to the sales history of the book. I can tell you things we were witness to—the things we at St. Martin's did, and what we *saw* other people do—but I still suspect that some effectively invisible event in a faraway exotic locale—like St. Louis or Chicago—changed the whole course of things unbeknownst to any of us. Given that caveat, I'll now describe the making of a bestseller by James Herriot.

When I first gathered round me the sympathetic faithful at St. Martin's to tell them what this wonderful new book I'd bought was about, the first thing I said was, "It's the memoirs of a doctor!" and everyone beamed. And then I added, "Of course, he's not a people doctor, he's an animal doctor," and their looks began to change. And then I added, "Of course, it's not really the memoirs, it's only two years." And I added that the two years weren't current, and my final subtraction, that the setting was not Kansas or Connecticut, but Yorkshire England. I was confronted with a sight I hope none of you ever has to behold, and that is a dozen of your closest friends walking away from you sideways. "Come back!" I shouted to them. "It's going to be a bestseller! My wife says so!"

I first encountered the writing of James Herriot on a buying trip to London. I was in the office of a London agent who had barely heard of St. Martin's and had never heard of me, so was not eager to offer me any property of certain value. Out of courtesy, he presented me with a 192 page, obviously long-published book called *If Only They Could Talk*. The agent had the grace to give me a sick half smile, to which I supplied the other half. "Looks like fun!" I lied, and headed back to America where the book lay on my bedside radio at home for a full three months, constantly elbowed aside by more likely manuscripts. My wife first read the book, and she said to me in the soft-spoken way I've learned to listen to, "You gotta read this and if you don't publish it, you booby, I'll kill you." So I read it and loved it. I won't try to convey to you the quality of James Herriot's writing beyond saying that he is a kind of story-writing genius. *All Creatures* is no more merely a barnyard memoir about pigs with measles than *Death of a Salesman* is merely a play about the damn New England territory.

I wanted to publish Herriot, but I wasn't sure about this particular book. As a milieu book, it was too short, and it didn't end, it just stopped. The agent informed me that another one had just been published, and handed me *It Shouldn't Happen to a Vet,* a book with a cartoon on the cover. Another unsalable job of packaging, I thought. This one, too, just stopped. However, he had met the girl, and they were courting. I needed still more—but not a third volume's worth, so I asked that the author write three more chapters—marry the girl and give me an ending. Herriot wrote the three chapters, gave us a wedding and an ending that chimes as gloriously as "The Sound of Music."

So we had our book. Now we needed a title. I wrote again to my vet, asking if he would suggest an alternative title. Meanwhile, we compiled lists at St. Martin's. The one that stood out was from the hymn: "All things bright and beautiful / All creatures great and small,/ All things wise and wonderful, / The Lord God made them all."

We talked James out of his proposed title, *Ill Creatures Great and Small,* and into ours. The job of packaging was done, and the job of marketing began.

The premise of the marketing effort was that this was a totally irresistible read, if only we could get people to start the thing. We had to get people—meaning reviewers, book buyers, and librarians—

started on the book. We could devise no descriptive copy that was as persuasive as we thought it ought to be. We raved, called it great, warm, rich, joyful, a miracle between covers, but every publisher raves, and every reader would see he was being asked to take seriously what seemed like just another animal book. Also, we realized that the book itself was its own best salesman. From the very first page, it is irresistible. If we could just get the first seven-page chapter into people we figured we had them hooked, so our campaign became one of enticement, intimidation, and force-feeding.

First, we made *All Creatures* the lead book in the fall catalog, the fall list announcement ad in *Publishers Weekly* and in our presentation at the ABA (now BookExpo America). Then we printed 6000 copies of the first chapter and gave them away—2000 at the ABA, and the rest by mail to librarians, bookstores and selected reviewers. We also sent it to assorted magazines, including all the veterinary journals we could find, telling them they could print it for free. This last, which seemed clever at the time, both worked and didn't work. None of them printed it—until after it became a bestseller.

The pre-pub reviews were strongly favorable, so we went back to *PW* with a two-page ad that quoted the reviews, detailed the ad campaign, and offered a triple-your-value-back guarantee for the book-store owner to offer any Scrooge that claimed he didn't like the book. We announced that multiple ads would be appearing in New York, Chicago, Washington, San Francisco, Philadelphia, Los Angeles, Detroit, Boston, St. Louis, Cleveland, Atlanta, Denver, Minneapolis, Milwaukee, Houston, Seattle, two veterinarian nationals, and half a dozen Christmas catalogs. The initial space-ad commitment was for just under $25,000. This was meant to be reassuring to bookstores and intimidating to reviewers. Next, we sent out little ivory animals to major bookstore buyers and big reviewers to remind them of the book, and followed up with phone calls.

But I still wasn't convinced that reviewers would look at it, so I decided to try a personal letter from me. I write such a letter maybe once a year—no more. I described the book's virtues and then said: "No book I've worked on in fifteen years of publishing has given me more pleasure." You can see why I try not to write a letter like that more than once a year.

Publication date was November 14th. The advance sale, despite all our efforts, was disappointing: up until two weeks before publication, we still had only 8500 copies out there. Having done all we could, we sat back and waited for the reviews.

Aside from scattered notices around the country, there was only one major review in the whole month of November. Fortunately, the review we did get was the front page of the *Chicago Times Book World*. The headline cited our own flap copy, saying, "Miraculous not too strong a word." The review started out with the line "If there is any justice, *All Creatures Great and Small* will become a classic of its kind." Apparently, the reviewer, Alfred Ames, had gone into the *Book World* editor's office every three hours while he was reading the book and told him that if he didn't put it on the front page, Ames would have him impeached.

Immediately, large orders began coming in from Illinois. There were no other major reviews that month. However, we took a full page ad in *The New York Times Book Review*, filling it with a copy of the *Book World* review.

The manager of Doubleday Bookshop in St. Louis called the senior buyer in New York and said that he must read the book. The buyer did, then checked the other Doubleday stores for customer reaction. Doubleday asked us to join them for a "big book" promotion—sharing a full page ad in the daily *Times*. We agreed, and they placed a large order. When Anatole Broyard gave the book a favorable review in *The New York Times*, Doubleday ordered another 5000 copies. On December 17, it made its first bestseller list in Chicago.

By January the flow of reviews was building. On the 21st, the *Houston Chronicle* headed its review "Superlatives Aren't Enough." On February 4th, *three months* after publication, *The Los Angeles Times* reviewed it. So did Maurice Dolbier of the *Providence Journal*; he titled his "One That Almost Got Away," and confessed that he hadn't taken the book home to read until he saw all the attention it was getting elsewhere. Other February reviews included *Time* magazine and the Sunday *New York Times Book Review.*

On January 8th it made *Time* magazine's national bestseller list, and on January 21st it first hit *TBR*'s list. At the end of February we brought James Herriot over from England for a week and he proved to be a marvelous television personality. In fact, we knew the book was scheduled to drop off the *TBR* bestseller list the week after he was here. He appeared on The Today Show, Mike Douglas, Kennedy and Co., and lots more in the one week. Whether or not it was cause and effect I don't know, but the book came back on the list a week later and stayed there for another dozen weeks.

The book has been a national bestseller for four and a half months. It has sold 80,000 copies and it's still, at this writing, selling at an extraordinarily steady rate of 3500 copies a week.

I'm sure the book has made it. But I'm still not altogether sure of the *making* of it. As of this moment we have spent $51,000 on promotion. I'm positive the reviews played the big role in the making of the book, and though I believe that our promotion prompted certain reviewers to look at it, the book itself—the author—has to get credit for the quality and impact of all those reviews.

We did not advertise the book after February and it was not being reviewed anymore, so I think the continuing sale has to be credited to word-of-mouth and the appearance on the bestseller list. We did spend money, and we hit every button we could see, but I still feel, shakily, that if it weren't for a man named Alfred Ames, it all might have turned out different.

Thomas J. McCormack
Former CEO, St. Martin's Press

A Journey through the Grassroots

The Story behind *The Twelve Gifts of Birth*

One morning in 1987, when my daughters were teenagers nearing high school graduation, I woke with shock. My children were about to leave home; the most critical years of their development were over; and I was just beginning to understand that unconditional love is the most important thing I could give them. With hindsight, I wished I had done some things differently.

Weeks later, once again I woke one day with strong emotion. This time it was a feeling of euphoria. In the sleep state, I had been in a place where I heard about twelve gifts. I remembered a few of them: Strength...Courage...Beauty...Compassion...Joy; and I recalled a repeated phrase *May you...May you...May you*...with what felt like a bestowing of blessings. As I moved into wakefulness, the details of a dream evaporated. Holding on to wisps of it, I wrote a message and fashioned into a booklet titled *Welcome to the World: The Twelve Gifts of Birth*. It was what I wished I had whispered in my babies' ears and said often as they grew. It told them they were born with gifts. Gentle wishes suggested how to use each gift to live well. I regretted that I had not articulated the message earlier and used it to guide my daughters. But I was just beginning to comprehend it myself.

I felt strongly that all children, not just my own, deserve to hear that they are worthy and gifted. I wanted to see *The Twelve Gifts of Birth* published. With high hopes, I prepared submission packages. After the 20th rejection, I decided to give up, not on publishing altogether, but on selling *The Twelve Gifts of Birth* to an established publisher. I resolved to publish it myself *someday*. For years *someday* was a vague, elusive time in the future. In 1995, I became increasingly disturbed by news stories of abused children. I realized that the message of *The*

Twelve Gifts of Birth held potential to help in a small way, and my resolve strengthened. But still I said *someday*.

A year later my mother's health deteriorated. Sitting in her quiet hospital room one afternoon, I heard a voice within me say *What you do with your time and talent is critically important. Pay attention.* I knew immediately what the admonition to *Pay attention* meant. It was time to embrace *someday* and act upon what was calling me—my book.

My mother died a month later. As soon as I could complete existing projects and fulfill commitments, I told my boss I was leaving recruiting to become a publisher. He encouraged me to follow my dream *someday* but "not yet," rationalizing that I probably needed a lot more cash than I had to start a business. I tried to conceal the fear and doubt I was feeling in that moment. I knew that, in a way, he was right. I had a nest egg of only $5,000. Still, I decided *someday* had arrived.

So I left a secure job and became a student of the small press industry, joining organizations like Arizona Book Publishing Association and Publisher's Marketing Association. I attended seminars and read everything I could about self-publishing. I conducted market research and gathered feedback on my little book from local booksellers and gift store owners. I went to BookExpo to find a distributor.

During the entire time I was learning and preparing *The Twelve Gifts of Birth* for publication, I experienced firsthand that miracles do happen when we follow our bliss in the spirit of service. When work is a labor of love, doors open. That was a premise and a promise that I had heard from many sources. And, although I believed it, never before had I acted as if it were true.

It took a year and half of full-time work and $50,000 to bring the richly-illustrated gift book into reality. *The Twelve Gifts of Birth* was released in September 1998, on National KidsDay®, a day intended to recognize the dignity of all children. In unexpected and surprising ways, all the resources that I needed along the way, financial and otherwise, appeared in perfect time. There were times when the steps I took seemed wrong or unnecessary, but later I saw how each "false" step became a stepping stone.

Months before printed books arrived, I sent announcement letters to friends and family. Their orders for multiple copies gave me much moral and some financial support. Twice that summer, my husband, Frank, and I packed up our Jeep with booth equipment and drove from our home in Phoenix to trade shows in the Midwest. We stood for days at gift shows in Denver and Chicago, offering everyone who passed our booth a card that contained the text of *The Twelve Gifts of Birth.* We asked buyers to read the short, 500-word message when they had some down time. Some people came back within a few minutes, some, a few hours; some, the next day. Many who returned came with moist eyes. But everyone who returned to our booth placed an order for a product yet to be printed.

When our first shipment of 5,000 books arrived, we filled orders. Within two weeks, we started receiving re-orders from gift stores - doubling, tripling, even quadrupling their initial orders. Within a few months we ordered a second, larger printing of 10,000 books.

I had anticipated that the book would do well, but the market's response surpassed my expectations. Many people wrote to say that the message expressed what they yearned to tell their children. Others shared how the book affected them. The first letter I received said, "I am seventy-two years old and have spent years of my life in therapy. I grew up believing that I was worthy only if I accomplished my goals and made a lot of money. My mind and heart have been healed by these twelve gifts. I realize that I live by them today but we both know they have been mine all along."

When I visited local schools and shelters and saw firsthand how eyes brighten when children hear the story, I wished I could do that throughout the country. But that seem like an impossible dream.

One Saturday afternoon, Frank and I saw an advertisement for a "colossal RV sale" and decided to take a look. After stepping in and out of a few models, we started to act like children playing, sitting in the driver and passenger seats and imagining new vistas and signs welcoming us to states we had not yet visited. After a while, we became quiet, explored models on our own, and looked at prices. On the way home, I said, "I have a crazy idea." Frank said, "Maybe it's not so crazy."

We mused over the possibilities of giving up our home, living in a motor home, and Frank taking a sabbatical from consulting. I could read and discuss the message with thousands of children, promote the book, and we could see the country.

The seemingly impossible dream became plausible when a special sales company called to negotiate a large order and ended up purchasing 225,000 copies. Although they paid only a small amount per book over print costs, it financed our trip and allowed Frank to leave his work for a year and focus fully what was fast becoming *our* mission.

Before buying a motor home, I called a best selling author who had used one to promote his book. His advice to me was "Don't do it! Imagine your house in an earthquake every day. That is what it sometimes feels like when you are traveling down the highway."

I then called the president of a small press company who had also used a motor home to market a bestseller. He offered some encouragement but counseled me that even a regional tour takes an immense amount of planning, coordination, and follow-up. He had a whole staff working on it. Did I?

Despite the cautions, we went ahead and moved from 2,500 square feet of living space into 250. On a sweltering summer Sunday in July

1999, we merged on I-10 in Phoenix and began a one year journey throughout the US. Frank gripped the wheel with intense focus while I watched the white lines. On both sides of our vehicle the lines seemed dangerously close, too easy to cross. *In setting out on this mission, had we crossed a line?* I wondered.

After a while our tense muscles eased a bit. We even started to sing until suddenly we heard a pop, felt a jarring shift, and smelled ruptured rubber. My stomach clenched. *A flat tire at forty miles into a 40,000 mile trip? Are we making a big mistake? Maybe that author was right.*

In many ways both the author and publisher were right. There were many challenges. The balancing jacks came down while we were driving. Low clearance bridges forced detours. On our way to Salt Lake City, on the day the first ever-recorded tornado hit the city, high winds ripped away one of our awnings. Pipes froze during a cold night in West Virginia. There were many challenges with email, regular mail and telephone communication. We often climbed to the roof for cell phone connection. Water leaked through the roof onto our computer during a heavy rainstorm and destroyed data. Forwarded snail mail sometimes got lost.

Creating a schedule was hard; following it was harder. Days were long. TV interviews, when I could get them, were on early morning shows. In late morning and early afternoon, we visited schools and shelters. Bookstore events started at 7:00 PM. We often didn't get situated on a site, hooked up, and in bed until very late. Then, all too often, the roar, whistle, and thundering vibration of a nearby train caused a sleepless night. Fortunately, we were safe and could usually laugh at the adventure of it all. Always, the positives outweighed the negatives. Many nights, when we were able to camp away from populated areas, we gazed at the star-studded sky and pondered our place in it all. We appreciated the diverse and magnificent American landscape as we drove from place to place, crossing mountains, rivers, plains, and prairies. We saw the sun sparkle on the Pacific, the Atlantic, and the Gulf of Mexico.

During the tour I became more aware both of the power within the human spirit and of human suffering. Every day, in addition to talking about the gifts, people disclosed their own struggles. Some stories were volunteered during group presentations, others were confided when I signed books. I am forever grateful and enriched by all the shared stories.

During that year, nearly 300,000 copies of *The Twelve Gifts of Birth* were sold; the book received attention in *Publishers Weekly* and it was recommended by BookSense. *The Twelve Gifts* message was licensed for use on a poster and a baby blanket. In July 2000, on the very last day of the tour, I received a call from an agent, offering to help me sell rights to a large publisher.

In 2001, *The Twelve Gifts of Birth* was re-released through HarperCollins Publishers in both English and Spanish, and has been followed by *The Twelve Gifts for Healing* and *The Twelve Gifts in Marriage*. *The Twelve Gifts of Birth* is also available in Japanese. The book continues to sell well and is being used in many ways by educators, therapists, clergy, and social workers. Several hospitals have decorated their birthing center walls with the message of *The Twelve Gifts of Birth*. A short film based on the book is being created for educational and inspirational use. For more information, visit *www.thetwelvegifts.com*.

Charlene Costanzo
Author, The Twelve Gifts of Birth

Blind Faith and Serendipity

One Author's Unlikely Journey from Self-Publishing to the Viking Frontlist

The story of how *Dear Zoe* found its way to Viking is one I still have trouble believing. If you have ever doubted the combined powers of blind persistence and serendipity, then read on.

After practicing law full-time for eleven years, I began work on my first novel, billing just enough hours from home to make family grocery money. Fueled mostly by fear, I finished it in nine months, and a year later secured a wonderful agent, Jane Dystel, to represent it. I was still naïve enough to believe that agents were magic, that a book deal was now imminent, and that the transition from my old career to my new one was complete. Six months and twenty-seven rejection letters later, *The Love Number* went back in the drawer. Fortunately, I had followed Jane's advice and was already halfway through a first draft of a second novel, and by January, 2003, *Dear Zoe* was ready for submission.

After the first six rejection letters arrived, I was advised by more than one person that I should change the point of view before submitting to any more publishers—that the epistolary format of *Dear Zoe* took away from the intimacy between narrator and reader and should be re-thought. I had resisted that advice for months, but, having already had one novel rejected by every major house in New York, I was willing to do just about anything to avoid the same fate for the second. I spent a month revising the novel to standard first person, changed the title to *Z*, then sat and cried when I sent it off that way.

The change didn't help. Three months later, the last of the twenty-eight rejection letters arrived. We came close more than once (I will always be indebted to Reagan Arthur at Little, Brown for her encouragement and for championing *Z* at that fine house), but in the end I was faced with the prospect of starting work on a third novel without any faith that it would find a home. I couldn't do it. Knowing that others had found success with their third or fourth books didn't help. I felt lost, directionless, paralyzed by the first real failure of my life. I couldn't picture myself going back to the practice of law full-time, yet three attempts to start a new novel went nowhere. I spent the spring and summer performing mindless tasks: I worked for my younger brother (the ultimate humiliation), finishing the new wood paneling in his basement, getting slightly looped on polyurethane; I went to the gym; got the yard in shape; I spent too much time watching the war in Iraq on CNN; I cleaned and alphabetized all 800 beer cans from the childhood collection that had been rusting in my parents' attic for 25 years; I wore out two pairs of sneakers walking the dog. Then I saw an article in the New York Times about self-publishing and decided to take back control of my new career.

I spent the next six months treating the publication of *Dear Zoe* as my full-time job. I went back to the earlier version of the manuscript — restoring both the original title and the original point of view — and read every text on self-publishing I could find. I formed Van Buren Books as a Pennsylvania LLC, solicited competing bids from small printers who took the time to teach me the difference between smythe sewn and adhesive case bindings, gloss and lay-flat matte lamination, headbands, footbands, endsheets, and binder boards. I found a cover designer (Amy King), a national distributor willing to take a chance on the book (Midpoint Trade Books), a tireless, imaginative publicist (Maryglenn McCombs), and I sent the manuscript to every published writer I had ever met (and some I hadn't) asking them to read *Dear Zoe* and consider providing a blurb for the back cover.

The key to finding all of these crucial contributors was, quite simply, not being afraid to ask. I knew my chances of success were minuscule, but I was energized by the ability to control every aspect of the process, by creating and following every small lead. For example, I found Amy King by taking fifty of my favorite covers off my shelves, checking the flaps for the designer credits, and stacking each designer in individual piles (you'd be surprised how few cover designers there are in New York). My wife and I agreed that Amy's covers were consistently the strongest, and I called Doubleday the next day looking for her. I was told that Amy no longer worked there, but that her husband was still with Random House. I asked to be transferred to him, and then found myself in New York Publishing Limbo — the secretary's voice mail — leaving a long meandering message about why I was looking for "your boss's wife." Incredibly, Amy King called me the next day. Pregnant with her second child, she had just left Doubleday to open her own design shop and was looking for new clients.

My agent, Jane Dystel, was invaluable during this time as well. I was afraid she was going to caution me that self-publishing would be akin to literary suicide, but she was supportive from the beginning. She put me in touch with tough publicity veteran, Rick Frishman, who gave me more of his time than I could have hoped for, along with some honest, sage advice that went something like this: "You're insane, you know; but if you insist on doing this, you'll need a distributor." He directed me to Eric Kampmann, President of Midpoint Trade Books, and if Eric initially took me on as a favor to Rick, he gradually became a vocal and active advocate for my novel. Eric, in turn, sent me to Maryglenn, my publicist. I had galleys produced at Express Media in Nashville using Amy King's design, and I settled on Thompson-Shore in Michigan to print 3,000 hardcover books. The project was really moving along nicely, even gathering a little momentum. But to finish the story, I first need to go back.

Just after deciding to self-publish, I was in my favorite independent bookstore, The Aspinwall Bookshop, two blocks from my home. When I was in law school, the proprietor, John Towle, had worked for a Pittsburgh indie bookseller institution, Jay Dantry of Jay's Bookstall, alongside then-Pitt writing student, Michael Chabon. I came to know John not just as someone who sold books, but as someone who recommended great books. Completely by chance, when I graduated from law school and moved to Aspinwall, John left Jay's and, after an interim location or two, opened his own one-room shop on my street. When I started writing again, John became the first unbiased barometer of my work.

The day I stopped by to tell John about my self-publishing plans, he told me that his Penguin sales rep, Jason Gobble, was due to stop in later that week, and that Jason was someone who "has some credibility with the editors at Penguin." I told John that the book had already been rejected by most of the Penguin imprints, but agreed to drop off a copy of the manuscript the next day.

A few months later, John called to tell me that Jason loved *Dear Zoe* and wanted permission to send it to Viking. I agreed but with no expectations. I had already wallpapered my office with rejection letters from New York, and I was certain this was going to be one more. What I was excited about, however, was the possibility of having an influential regional sales rep behind my book. Jason Gobble and I struck up an e-mail friendship, and although he couldn't "officially" represent my book to the independents in his five-state territory, he agreed to distribute my galleys informally to all of his best hand-sellers with a strong recommendation.

Just weeks after sending my manuscript off to Viking, Jason Gobble was named by Publishers Weekly as its Sales Rep of the Year and was featured in a three-page spread. Suddenly, Van Buren Books and *Dear Zoe* had a very influential advocate. Over the course of the next couple of months, I increased my planned print run to 5,000 copies, and Maryglenn and Midpoint both scheduled signings for me at the

BookExpo in Chicago in June, 2004. I had 100 galley copies printed for distribution through Jason to booksellers, through Maryglenn to reviewers, and through Midpoint to their national account reps, and Amy King and I finalized the jacket design. During that time, I honestly never gave a thought to the Viking submission.

On March 23, 2004, I was sitting at my computer, corresponding with Amy King on the final jacket layout. The overall design had been set for weeks, but we had been struggling with the logo for Van Buren Books that would appear on the spine. To stay within my publication timeline, we needed to have the final design mechanicals to our printer within a couple of days. At the same time, I would write the largest check of my life to print books I couldn't be sure anyone beyond my Christmas card list would buy. I sent an e-mail to Amy with my final decision on the logo, instructing her to get the mechanicals to the printer by the next day. Then I called Maryglenn, confirmed that we were on schedule, and told her to start sending the galleys out to the advance reviewers. When I clicked back to my in-box, there was an e-mail from the receptionist at my law firm that said the following:

"Clare Ferraro from Viking called and would like you to call her back. She said to say she works with Jason Gobble."

I stared at that message, motionless, for what must have been a full minute. I knew that Clare Ferraro didn't just "work with Jason Gobble," that she was the president of Viking Penguin. And although I couldn't imagine how a call from her could possibly be bad news, it just didn't seem possible that, after four years, a novel of mine was going to find a home in New York on the same day I was finalizing plans to print it myself. Of course, that's exactly what happened. By the end of the day, Jane Dystel had come to an agreement with Viking, and I had notified everyone involved in my self-publishing effort that Van Buren Books was suspending operations. Three weeks later, *Dear Zoe* appeared in the "Hot Deals" column of *Publishers Weekly*. Unbelievable.

Still, I am probably the only writer who ever felt a sense of nostalgia along with the elation of finally being validated by New York. In the process of preparing *Dear Zoe* to go to press, I came to know every player in the chain of production, promotion, and distribution in a way that can never happen at a major publishing house; nor should it. The people at Viking have done more for *Dear Zoe* than I could ever have hoped to do on my own. For the month of its release in April, 2005, *Dear Zoe* was both a Book Sense Pick and a Borders "Original Voices" selection. An audio version, as read by actress Cassandra Morris, was released simultaneously by Highbridge audio and won an AudioFile "Earphones" Award. More recently, *Booklist* named *Dear Zoe* one of the Ten Best First Novels of 2005, and it was selected as a BookSense Summer Paperback for the summer of 2006. And remember that first novel that went into the drawer? Viking purchased that one as well and published *Lost in the Garden* in May, 2006.

Fortunately, I have been able to continue my relationship with many of the people I worked with in my self-publishing effort: Amy King was retained by Viking to work on its version of the *Dear Zoe* cover; Maryglenn McCombs still e-mails me with sage promotional advice; Jason Gobble got to sell the novel he discovered in the tiny Aspinwall Bookshop until he moved on to a new job with Ingram; and John Towle, the owner of that shop and always the first person outside my family to read my work, hosted my first official book signing and has sold more copies of both of my novels than any other bookseller in the country.

Philip Beard
Author, Dear Zoe and Lost in the Garden

MARKET, MARKET, MARKET!
BUILDING A BRAND THAT LASTS

Robert Kiyosaki is no overnight sensation. Many people first heard of his best selling book *Rich Dad, Poor Dad: What the Rich Teach Their Kids About Money – That the Poor and Middle Class Do Not!* when he appeared on Oprah a couple of years ago. The book is the story of Kiyosaki's "two dads" and what each taught him about money. The Rich Dad was Kiyosaki's best friend's father, and the person most responsible for teaching him what the rich know about managing money. Kiyosaki's Poor Dad, his own father, was a government worker who struggled with his finances his entire life. Before that big break, Kiyosaki had put in years of practice learning how to sell himself and his message quickly and effectively. He honed his skills on radio programs, TV programs, and by presenting on stage. As Kiyosaki's Rich Dad said, "If you want to be successful in business, you must learn how to sell."

While *Rich Dad, Poor Dad* is probably his best-known title (10 million copies in print, translated into almost 35 languages), Kiyosaki has slowly built an information empire with other titles that focus on a variety of specific economic concepts, as well as board games, audio and videotape series, and a line of Rich Dad Advisor products. Here are some strategies that Kiyosaki used to build his empire:

• **Create controversy**. You might think that part of becoming a best selling author involves cultivating an adoring public. But that's not the way Kiyosaki sees it. In fact, he says that if you're doing your job right, only about 33% of the public is going to love you, with the other two-thirds split evenly between hating you and being indifferent. The reason is because one of the keys to success is controversy—and that is necessarily going to mean ruffling some feathers and making some people downright antagonistic to your message. But controversy makes for a good story, good stories attract media attention, and media attention sells books.

• **Kill the sacred cow**. How do you go about creating the kind of controversy that grabs the media's attention? Take a generally accepted belief and challenge it. For example, while most homeowners view their house as an asset, Kiyosaki argues just the opposite. In his Rich Dad's world, anything (like your house) that doesn't produce income and that requires you to make payments on it every month can only be considered a liability. As you can imagine, there are plenty of people who didn't like hearing that about the biggest investment of their lives. As Kiyosaki puts it, marketing is like "drawing a line in the sand"—people are either going to agree with what you're saying or they won't. But either way, it's going to attract attention.

• **Make it simple**. In a nutshell, the harder you make it for people to understand the message, the less likely they are to want to buy your book. Kiyosaki's forte is taking the complicated and making it simple. (Most people do just the opposite). Kiyosaki has found that this also makes your message more appealing to the media. If you can't convey the essence of your topic and your most intriguing points in just a few seconds, most people aren't going to wait around to figure out what you're trying to say. And remember, the media loves sound bites.

• **Appeal to a person's spirit**. Kiyosaki's message is powerful for a variety of reasons, not the least of which is the fact that it appeals to one of the most deep-seated desires of most of us: to be financially independent. Kiyosaki has often said, "It's not about making money, it's about being free." It's obvious Kiyosaki has hit an international chord with *Rich Dad, Poor Dad,* making the bestseller lists not only in the United States but also in Japan, China, Korea, Taiwan, Singapore, Indonesia, South Africa, etc.

• **Focus just as much on your marketing as on your writing**. Kiyosaki stresses that he isn't a best *writing* author, he's a best *selling* author. In fact, Kiyosaki doesn't consider himself a particularly talented writer at all. But what he *can* do is sell. In his youth, Kiyosaki took a job hawking copiers to overcome his fear of selling. It's a skill that pays off to this day. Think about what you do to market your books—you sell yourself to the media, to bookstores, to reviewers, to producers and so on. Knowing how to write is one piece of the puzzle, but knowing how to sell and market your message may be even more important.

• **Be ready for Oprah's call**. According to Kiyosaki, about 99% of authors aren't ready for the dream phone call from one of Oprah's producers. As a result, even a guest spot on one of the most widely watched TV shows in America won't catapult them to bestseller status. The only way to get ready for that call is to practice your media skills, your presentation skills and how to get your message across most effectively. Kiyosaki has done hundreds of radio and TV interviews (many of which were a result of ads he placed in *Radio-TV Interview Report*, the magazine producers read to find guests) and spoke to live audiences throughout the world in preparation for the day when he got his shot on Oprah. That chance came when Kiyosaki was on vacation in the Australian outback on a hunting expedition. After getting the call, he immediately hopped on a plane and flew directly to Chicago for the appearance. Because of the time he spent practicing and his willingness to go the extra mile (or extra few thousand miles, in this case) Kiyosaki attributes selling a million copies of his book to his first Oprah appearance.

• **Create high-profit spin-offs**. It's much, much easier (and cheaper for you) if a single customer buys several of your products instead of you constantly recruiting new customers to buy just one product. In other words, if someone buys your $19.95 book and likes it, there's a good chance they'll be interested in your $99.95 audiotape set, or your $199.95 videotape set. Kiyosaki is a believer in this system and created his spin-offs (also known as back-end products) before he ever wrote his book. Essentially, he wrote his book *Rich Dad, Poor Dad* to help him sell a $195 game called *CASHFLOW® 101*. Don't stop with just one product. If people are responding to your message then why not offer them additional products that give them more information while simultaneously increasing your profit margin?

• **Zero in on niche markets**. When Kiyosaki learned that multi-level marketing companies (MLMs) were buying his books and encouraging their associates to read them, he contacted various MLM companies and asked them what they wanted. As a result, he wrote an entire book for them, titled *The Business School for People Who Like Helping People* and sold hundreds of thousands of copies *just* to various MLMs. This is taking the concept of the "special report" several steps further. If you can identify a niche market that would benefit from a specialized version of your book, why not create something tailored just for them? It might be a booklet, a training manual, a tape series or, if the market is big enough like it was for Kiyosaki, an entirely new book. All of Kiyosaki's books include ads at the back for higher-priced games and audio tapes, which range in price from $149 to $295. Many book buyers purchase one or more of these "back-end" products — sales which are very profitable because there's almost no advertising cost.

• **Build a brand**. The *Rich Dad* brand is, if not a household name, at least known by enough people that Kiyosaki has been able to expand on his initial product line to offer specialized titles on the subjects of real-estate investing, sales, and tax strategies written by other authors but published under the "Rich Dad" umbrella (the Rich Dad Advisor Series). Like all brands, these products are all instantly recognizable as being part of the same family. Thus, if you liked what Kiyosaki had to say in *Rich Dad, Poor Dad*, chances are you'll be interested in these other topics.

For more information about Robert Kiyosaki, *Rich Dad, Poor Dad*, or any of his other products, visit *www.richdad.com.*

Steve Harrison
Creator of Radio-TV Interview Report
www.freepublicity.com

The Power of a Postcard

Using the News to Build Sales

A recent article in *Publishers Weekly* reported about an author who shot their book up to the #1 spot on Amazon.com where it remained for two days. This new marketing tactic (called "permission marketing") is becoming very popular.

Unfortunately, it's not inexpensive *and* you must also have access to a large database of email addresses. This database is blasted with persuasive emails about buying your book. If you have the database and funds to do this, great! You can get your book to the #1 spot on Amazon. Whether it stays there for one day or one week, you can now call yourself a best selling author.

Challenging the traditional is the only way to get noticed in a noisy world and there are other ways to launch that challenge. That's how I got my first book, *The Cliffhanger*, to the #1 spot on Amazon.com (best selling book within San Diego) where it stayed for three months. How did I do it?

I hung my star on something already in the public eye: the 2000 Presidential election. You remember that, right? How could you forget?! In the midst of chads, hanging and otherwise, our local paper ran a huge headline that read: CLIFFHANGER! I knew if I couldn't find a way to position my book around that, I needed to hang up my marketing hat. Problem: *The Cliffhanger* had *nothing* to do with politics. It was a love story about people in denial. (No news there.) Still, I knew if I looked hard enough, I could find a way.

I woke that night at 3:00 AM with an idea so outrageous, I knew it had to work. I raced out to the office supply store the minute it opened to pick up several packs of clear labels. I got out the postcards I had printed with the book cover on them and stuck on labels with the following slogan:

Getting tired of the Presidential cliffhanger?
Try this one.
***The Cliffhanger*, a novel.**
No politics involved.

I mailed 500 postcards out that day while praying the election wouldn't get called. I mailed these postcards to everyone in the media I'd ever contacted. Ever!

Days after my mass-mailing, I was walking through my living room when suddenly I spotted my book cover on the screen. I was stunned. The local TV anchor was saying, "This has got to be the best thing I've ever seen. This lady wants you to go buy her book. I say everyone should rush out and buy it." And everyone did. That afternoon my book shot up to the #1 spot on Amazon where it stayed for three months. It even beat out Harry Potter (which was #4 at that time) yet Harry got the movie. Go figure.

That single postcard shot my book up the ranks at Amazon and quite literally changed my life and the way I look at marketing. To this day, people in the industry still know me as *The Cliffhanger* lady. And I'm happy and proud about that.

This week, I charge you to do something outrageous in your campaign. Challenge the norm. Step outside the book and rise above the noise. Remember, sometimes it takes only one thing—just one thing to make a difference.

Wishing you an outrageously successful campaign!

Penny C. Sansevieri
Author, The Cliffhanger and
Red Hot Internet Publicity
www.amarketingexpert.com

EXPANDING YOUR HORIZONS

SELLING BEYOND THE BOOKSTORES

After being laid off my job in corporate America, I decided to start a new business as an author and publisher. My first thought was, H*ow hard could it be to write, publish, and market a book*? I soon found out.

I began my writing career seeking a topic 1) for which there was a large audience, 2) for which there was proven demand, and 3) on which I had vast experience. Given this criteria I wrote and self-published the title *Job Search 101,* which describes basic, creative techniques for getting a job. I found a distributor, was accepted by Borders and Barnes & Noble, and sat back waiting for the checks to begin flowing in.

It was not long before I was selling many books, but was not making significant profits. It was then that I learned about the concepts of distribution discounts, returns, and 120-day payment terms. So I looked for places to sell books where these concepts did not apply. That was the first time I heard about *special sales* (non-bookstore marketing) and learned several important lessons about selling books profitably.

Lesson 1: Find new markets

At the time, there was significant need for job-search information among many different audiences. I defined my target readers to include state governments, college students, Latinos, and released corporate employees. Armed with these new opportunities, I hunted sales in segments my competitors ignored: state governments, colleges, Latinos, and corporate HR people.

Lesson 2: Provide your information in a different format

The form of the product that delivers your information is flexible and may be modified to best serve the needs of the user. For example, research among college students determined that they wanted job-search information in a cheaper, easier-to-use format. So I converted the content of *Job Search 101* into a series of eight 32-page booklets.

With a little re-writing, the booklets were easily adapted to meet the needs of state governments where agencies conduct workshops for their constituents. They usually refrain from buying bound books because they do not easily lie flat. I increased my sales significantly by publishing *Job Search 101* with a spiral binding that was easy to use during these workshops.

Another example of offering information in a different format was my video, *The Art of Interviewing*. In this case, the job-search interviewing techniques of correct posture, eye communication, gesturing, and voice control were more easily communicated in a video format than in writing.

Lesson 3: Find new users for your existing information

I discovered an absence of career information available for the Hispanic market. Hence, I had *Job Search 101* translated into Spanish and published as *Elementos basicos para buscar trabajo*. This required a new distribution network, one more knowledgeable in servicing a market unfamiliar to the publisher.

It also helps to sub-divide each segment. For example, think of the library market. There are public libraries, academic libraries, corporate libraries, and religious libraries. I found that prison libraries needed a job-search book for prisoners about to be released. Libraries on military bases also needed my book to help prepare military personnel about to enter the job market. I also found more opportunities in the college market. In addition to selling *Job Search 101* to college career departments (at list price with no distributor discounts and no returns), I made additional sales to alumni groups, college libraries, and instructors of job-search courses looking for a textbook.

Lesson 4: Find new uses for your basic information

Many of the skills required to interview for a job are required by authors to perform on television and radio shows. I re-purposed the interview techniques of correct posture, eye communication, facial gestures, body language, and voice control to create the media-training video program, *You're on the Air*. I also wrote its two companion guides, *Perpetual Promotion* and *It's Show Time* to extend this initial product offering.

Lesson 5: Implement creative promotional campaigns

The marketing technique of *bundling* occurs when two or more associated products are packaged together and sold as one item. I employed this tactic in a direct-mail campaign directed to the parents of graduating college students with a *bundle* comprised of *The Art of Interviewing* and *Job Search 101* offered at a discounted price.

If you pursue sales in non-bookstore market segments you should be able to prolong the profitable life of your original title while creating additional revenue in other contexts. Learn from all the lessons describe above and you can significantly increase your income in the marketing process called *special sales.*

Brian Jud
Author, Job Search 101
www.bookmarketingworks.com

APPENDICES

APPENDIX A
Tips for Successful Book Marketing & Promotion

Groucho Marx may have said it best when he said, "Outside of a dog, a book is a man's best friend. Inside of a dog, it's too dark to read." Too often, publishers and authors are "in the dark" about how to effectively promote and publicize a book.

Whether you are an experienced author or publisher or completely new to the publishing business, you probably know you have to create awareness in order to create demand for a book. To create awareness, you have to promote your book. Effectively promoting a book is a combination of timing, creativity, contacts and luck, but these tips can help you maximize your book's potential.

1. Plan ahead.

Several front-end decisions can increase your book's chances of success. However, there are few things more important than the book's physical packaging. Make sure that your book is professionally edited and designed. Also, resist the urge to overprice.

2. Know your market.

If you think the world at large is your market, you will probably never find it. Markets are specific and identifiable. Your book will always have a market but you must have it defined in order to reach it.

3. Develop a focused database.

This has tremendous value as these names can become repeat customers.

4. Create a website.

5. Set a realistic retail price for your book.

Your pricing must be competitive. Visit a bookstore to see how similar books are priced. Be objective. Even though you are passionate about the book, play the part of the skeptic. What would you pay for the book?

6. Attend local book fairs.

7. Keep going.

Do not get discouraged. Be optimistic.

8. Have a realistic marketing budget.

Whatever you do, don't spend all of your money just producing your book. How will prople know about your book if you don't have enough money budgeted to market it?

9. Promote yourself.

If you are an expert or authority who can comment on issues—particularly those in the news—let the media know. Become a source. Even if a journalist does not interview you right away, you may be kept on file as a source to contact in the future. Try to develop relationships with reporters concerning your area of expertise. If you can help the reporter, he or she may one day return the favor. Make sure you know, however, before you provide information whether you are "on" or "off" the record.

10. Enter your book in contests.

Awards can encourage additional sales and can also help with future books.

11. Research.

Before pitching a media outlet, do your research. Take note of editorial style, types of articles published or guests interviewed, topics frequently covered, lead-times and audience. Pitch accordingly.

12. No media outlet is too small.

Regardless of a media outlet's size, location or circulation, do not discriminate. If a media outlet is interested in your book or in interviewing you, accept the invitation. You never know who might be watching, listening or reading. Remember that alumni associations are always looking for interesting news about alums and may promote you for free.

13. Get bound galleys out early.

In addition to soliciting trade reviews with your galleys, you may also want to use them when seeking endorsements or blurbs for your book.

14. Send review copies out immediately after you receive finished copies.

15. Think beyond reviews

Too often, authors and publishers are so focused on getting reviews that they overlook other opportunities for book mentions and stories. Explore all angles, even if that means placing less emphasis on your book and greater emphasis on your story.

Be creative–think of ways your book's message ties in to a current issue, or relates to a trend. For instance, if your book explains how small businesses can take advantage of new tax codes, pitch a story explaining what small business owners need to know about new tax codes and time your pitch to coincide with the end of the year, when your advice would be most beneficial.

Focus on what is new or noteworthy about your book and how it can enlighten, entertain, or benefit the media outlet's audience. For example, if your book provides a groundbreaking strategy for selling in the new economy, pitch a story that shows how salespeople can use your strategy to earn higher commissions and make more sales.

16. Slow down!

Most importantly, do not try to do everything at once. Good book publicity campaigns take time and don't happen overnight. Relax, enjoy the process and have patience. Timing can be everything, so keep an eye on the news, on trends and happenings that may give you an opportunity to promote your book.

REMEMBER...

Every book should be launched as if it is a new business.

APPENDIX B
AUTHOR'S/ILLUSTRATOR'S QUESTIONNAIRE

Please fill out the following form. The information will be used in promoting and publicizing your book. Please return it, together with a photograph of yourself, to us. It is fine to e-mail the photo and completed questionnaire. Please note that credit must be given for the photograph. Please type or print. Thank you.

Date: ______________________

Name: ____

Legal Name (if different from above):_________________________

Address: ____

Home Phone: _____________________________

Home Fax: _______________________________

Office Address: _______________________________________

Office Phone: _____________________________

Office Fax: ______________________________

E-mail Address: _______________________________________

Website Address: _____________________________________

BIOGRAPHICAL INFORMATION:

Place of birth: ____

Citizenship: ____

Name of spouse: ______________________________________

Children (names, ages): _________________________________

____

____

Education: ____

____

Present title, department, and rank (if applicable): ______________

____

Professional organizations of which you are a member (note if you are or have been an officer or board member): ______________

____

____

Titles of other publications (indicate whether you were the author, editor, or contributor):

Title	Publisher	Year	Sales

Special Interests and Hobbies: ______________________

____

Relevant Travel: ______________________________

____

Brief biographical sketch (100-150 words): ______________

____

____

____

____

____

Family information which you want included in your author bio:

____

____

TITLE INFORMATION:

Full Working Book Title: ________________________

____

Subtitle: ____________________________________

____

ISBN-13: ______________________________

Binding: ______________________________

Publication Date: ______________________________

Please describe your book as if you were writing a book jacket or promotional piece for potential readers. Consider what is most important about your book, what special contributions it makes to your field, and what features, theoretical approach, data, photographs, etc., make it attractive to your audience (~250 words).

____

____

____

____

If there are other books on the same subject, how does your work differ from those books?

____

____

____

Audience and market for which this book is intended:

____

____

Please list any suggestions you have for promoting this book including sections of the country or localities which might have a particular interest in you or your book (i.e. local newspapers and bookstores): ______________________________

____

Please list special publications, critics, features writers, commentators, prominent individuals of your acquaintance, and professional or other groups who might be especially interested in your book or helpful in promoting it: ______________________________

____

____

Will you be available for (please check):
______ Newspaper interviews
______ Radio and television appearances
______ Speeches at schools, libraries, clubs, etc.

Would you mind being contacted directly by bookstores in your area for events/appearances? Is there anything in your book which you consider "newsworthy," which might make a newspaper story off the book pages?

Describe any special research or experience that contributed to this book:

GENERAL QUESTIONS:
What are some of your favorite books?

Favorite movies?

Why did you write the book you wrote?

How did you get the idea?

What was the hardest part?________________________________

____

____

What was the easiest part? ________________________________

____

____

On what authority did you write the book? ____________________

____

____

Please jot down several (5 to 10) questions you might like a reviewer or interviewer to ask you about your book:

____

____

____

____

____

Please list any endorsements/blurbs you have received regarding your book: _______________________________________

____

____

____

____

____

APPENDIX C
ADDITIONAL RESOURCES

PUBLISHING

101 Publishing Tips for Speakers and Consultants by Celia Rocks (Dottie Dehart), 2004, Pittsburgh Publishing & Company, Inc.

Damn! Why Didn't I Write That? How Ordinary People are Raking in $100,000.00...or More Writing Nonfiction Books & How You Can Too! by Marc McCutcheon, 2001, Quill Driver Books

Guerilla Advertising by Jay Conrad Levinson, 1994, Houghton Mifflin

How to Get Happily Published: A Complete and Candid Guide by Judith Appelbaum, Fourth Edition, 1996, HarperCollins

How to Get Your Book Published: Inside Secrets of a Successful Author by Robert W. Bly, 2000, Roblin Books

How to Start and Run A Small Book Publishing Company: A Small Business Guide To Self-Publishing And Independent Publishing by Peter I. Hupalo, 2002, HCM Publishing

Publishing for Profit: Successful Bottom-Line Management for Book Publishers by Thomas Woll, 2002, Cross River Publishing Consultants, Inc.

Self-Publishing 101 by Debbie Elicksen, 2005, Self Counsel Press

Successful Nonfiction, Tips & Inspiration for Getting Published by Dan Poynter, 1999, Para Publishing

Is There a Book Inside You? Writing Alone or with a Collaborator by Dan Poynter, et al., 1998, Para Publishing

Author 101: Bestselling Secrets from Top Agents by Rick Frishman and Robyn Freedman Spizman, 2006, Adams Publishing Group

The Complete Guide to Self-Publishing by Tom & Marilyn Ross, *Revised fourth edition*, 2002, Writer's Digest Books

The Huenefeld Guide to Book Publishing by John Huenefeld, *Revised sixth edition*, 2002, Mills and Sanderson, Publishers

The Self-Publishing Manual: How to Write, Print and Sell Your Own Book by Dan Poynter, *Fourteenth Edition*, 2003, Para Publishing

The Shortest Distance Between You and a Published Book: 20 Steps to Success by Susan Page, 1997, Broadway Books

Writing Nonfiction: Turning Thoughts into Books by Dan Poynter, 2005, Para Publishing

Sales

Author 101: Bestselling Book Proposal: The Insider's Guide to Selling Your Work by Rick Frishman and Robyn Freedman Spizman, 2000, Adams Media

Beyond the Bookstore: How to Sell More Books Profitably to Non-bookstore Markets by Brian Jud, 2003, Reed Press

Jump Start Your Book Sales by Marilyn and Tom Ross, 1999, Writer's Digest Books

Editing

Self-Editing for Fiction Writers: How to edit yourself into print by Renni Browne & David King, Second edition, 2004, Harper Resource

The Marshall Plan for Getting Your Novel Published: 90 strategies and techniques for selling your fiction by Evan Marshall, 2003, Writer's Digest Books

Marketing

1001 Ways to Market Your Books by John Kremer, *Sixth Edition*, 2006, Open Horizons

Guerilla Marketing for Writers: 100 Weapons to Help You Sell Your Work by Jay Conrad Levinson, 2000, Writer's Digest Books

PUBLICITY AND PROMOTION

An Author's Guide to Children's Book Promotion by Susan Salzman Raab, *Ninth edition*, 2005, Raab Associates, Inc.

Author 101: Bestselling Book Publicity: The Insider's Guide to Promoting Your Book—and Yourself by Rick Frishman, 2006, Adams Publishing Group

Author 101: Bestselling Nonfiction: The Insider's Guide to Making Reality Sell by Rick Frishman, 2006, Adams Publishing Group

Guerrilla Publicity: Hundreds of Sure-Fire Tactics to Get Maximum Sales for Minimum Dollars by Rick Frishman, 2002, Adams Publishing Group

Publicize Your Book! An Insider's Guide to Getting Your Book the Attention It Deserves by Jacqueline Deval, 2003, A Perigee Book

The Savvy Author's Guide to Book Publicity by Lissa Warren, 2004, Carroll & Graph Publishers

Acknowledgments

The clear theme of this book has been the importance of collaboration, teamwork, and community in building a well-published book. This book is a perfect example. Many, many people have directly and indirectly contributed valuable information and advice that make up the essence of this handbook.

First, I want to express deep appreciation to my two partners. Both Gail Kump and Chris Bell were there at the beginning and both have been amazing contributors to the growth and success of Midpoint.

I want to particularly thank Gail for her invaluable contributions to the sales and distribution chapters of this book. I also want to thank the hundreds of independent publishers who have worked with Midpoint over the past ten years. As much as we would like to say that we played a vital role in their publishing activities, the truth is that they have taught us as much as we have taught them.

Jeanne Kramer, Ian Kimmich, Margot Atwell, and Gail Kearns contributed enormously to the accuracy, structure, and coherence of this book. I thank them for their hard work. Jeanne was particularly valuable because she brought a vision to this project that motivated everyone. I would also like to thank all those who have generously contributed essays to the book: Philip Beard, Charlene Costanzo, Steve Harrison, Brian Jud, Thomas McCormack, and Penny Sansevieri.

Others who played a role, both large and small, include: Tom Campbell, Sara Eisenman, Julie Hardison, Alex Kampmann, Vally Sharpe, Mark Kohut, Mark Levine, Laurie Little, David Nelson, Tony Outhwaite, Margaret Queen, John Teall, and many, many others.

Thank you all.

Index

Notes

Notes

Notes

NOTES

Notes